Retirement, Pensions, and
Social Security

Retirement, Pensions, and Social Security

Gary S. Fields
and
Olivia S. Mitchell

The MIT Press
Cambridge, Massachusetts
London, England

This book was set in Apollo by Asco Trade Typesetting Ltd., Hong Kong and printed and bound by Halliday Lithograph in the United States of America.

Library of Congress Cataloging in Publication Data

Fields, Gary S.
   Retirement, pensions, and social security.

   Bibliography: p.
   Includes index.
   1. Retirement—Economic aspects—United States. 2. Retirement income—United States.
3. Retirement—United States—Planning.   I. Mitchell, Olivia S.   II. Title.
HQ1062.F52   1984   306´.38´0973   84-11310
ISBN 0-262-06091-4

To Sophy and Milton, Marcia and Nat, Betty and Clyde, Louise and Bill

Contents

List of Figures

List of Tables

Acknowledgments

This book presents the findings of research begun in 1980. Our work was supported by many research organizations, donor agencies, and individuals. For providing a congenial research environment, we thank the Department of Labor Economics (New York State School of Industrial and Labor Relations) and the Department of Economics at Cornell University. In addition, the Department of Economics at the University of Warwick, England, generously housed Gary Fields for a term while at work on the project; Harvard University and the National Bureau of Economic Research served as a research base for Olivia Mitchell during a year on leave from Cornell. Financial assistance was provided by the U.S. Department of Labor's Pension and Welfare Benefits Program, which funded a major study on private pensions; the National Institute on Aging, which supported research on discrete choice retirement models; the National Commission on Employment Policy, which asked us to investigate Social Security reforms; and the host institutions themselves, which expended research funds on this project. Research assistants whose capable talents ensured the completion of the project on time included Jeff Avizinis, Gloria Bazzoli, Jorge Ducci, and Rebecca Luzadis. Special thanks go to Vivian Fields, whose programming skills, patience, and diligence made her an invaluable member of the research team. We also acknowledge the professionalism and good cheer of our secretary, Debbie Nivison.

Special appreciation goes to our colleagues Richard Ippolito and Emily Andrews for their encouragement through all stages of the research. Alan Gustman and Daniel Feenberg provided helpful comments and assistance; we thank them for many interesting discussions. Members of several research seminars provided comments on earlier stages of the work; these include participants in the Labor Workshop and the Social Insurance Seminar at Harvard University, and department seminars at Boston University, Brandeis University, the University of Chicago, Cornell University, North Carolina

State University, the University of Warwick, and Wellesley College, as well as various professional meetings and conferences. Several government officials were especially helpful in providing and analyzing data; particular thanks are due to Richard Ippolito and to members of his staff, including Daniel Beller, Ed Fu, Walter Kolodrubetz, and David McCarthy.

Finally, we acknowledge each other's contribution to this volume. The approach and conclusions in this book could have been produced by either of us working separately; indeed in articles published on this research, we have alternated first authorship, reflecting the equivalency of our contributions to the final product. By collaborating, we did the work more efficiently and we had more fun.

Introduction

American workers are retiring earlier, living longer, and receiving greater retirement benefits for each year out of the labor force than ever before, a situation that is creating serious financial pressures on the nation's retirement income system. In 1983 Congress was forced to raise Social Security taxes and lower Social Security benefits.[1] If Congress had not acted, Social Security checks would have stopped for 36 million recipients that summer.

These problems and others have generated an intense and often heated debate, with the merits of alternative benefit and financing schemes argued at many levels. People disagree for many reasons, including narrow self-interest or conflicting perceptions of social goals. What concerns us here is that contrary positions are often arrived at on account of different behavioral assumptions.

A case in point is the proposal put forth by the Reagan administration in 1981 that would have sharply reduced the Social Security benefits paid to retirees at age 62 but would have left benefits unchanged for workers who waited until 65 to collect Social Security. Supporters of this policy change contended that it would induce workers to delay retirement, helping the financially hard-pressed Social Security system in two ways: it would permit the system to pay benefits to fewer retirees and enable it to collect additional revenues during the prolonged work period. Critics reasoned otherwise. They argued that the elderly either would not work longer (because they did not want to) or could not work longer (because of poor health or unemployment). The primary consequence of the proposed reform, critics charged, would have been to render the elderly poorer, with the most adverse effect being felt by the least fortunate among them—those forced to retire earliest.

One important difference between the two camps was their different behavioral assumptions. The president's advisers assumed that older workers would alter their retirement behavior substantially in response to the changed structure of retirement income opportunities. Critics assumed that retirement ages would remain unchanged but retirees would receive less income. Which assumption is correct is an empirical matter about which little was known in 1981. The Reagan proposal died, but politics, not analytics, was reponsible.

In this book we examine this and other similar policy debates by asking two empirical questions: (1) What are the income opportunities facing older workers at alternate retirement ages? (2) How responsive are older workers' retirement ages to changes in income opportunities? We answer these questions by modeling the income opportunities facing older workers and estimating the effects of these economic factors on older workers' retirement decisions.[2]

We provide new empirical evidence on a number of major issues: the importance of such economic factors as earnings, private pensions, and Social Security benefits in relation to health, mandatory retirement, and other noneconomic factors in determining retirement patterns; the amounts of private pension and Social Security benefits that workers would receive at alternate retirement ages; the prospective budget sets facing potential retirees for retirement ages ranging from 60 to 68; variation across pension plans in the gains or losses from deferring retirement; regression models showing that retirement patterns can be explained in part by the retirement income streams available at a base age (age 60) and by the gain in retirement income if retirement is postponed from age 60 to age 65; multinomial logit and ordered logit models that formulate the retirement decision in a utility-based framework while accounting for unmeasured preferences of individuals and nonlinearities in income opportunities; predictions of the responsiveness of retirement ages and retirement incomes to reductions in Social Security benefits, using several different prediction methods, including one that is entirely new; and explanations for differences in average retirement ages among workers in different pension plans in terms of differences in the economic rewards for deferring retirement and differences in workers' tastes for income and leisure. Data are drawn from two sources: the Longitudinal Retirement History Survey, which has been used extensively by past researchers, and the Benefits Amounts Survey, a data set compiled by the U.S. Department of Labor and authorized for our use in the work reported here.

The analysis we report here represents a synthesis of four years of research using several different data sets and empirical frameworks. We take a microeconomic approach, casting retirement incomes and retirement choices in an intertemporal context, and examine how the choice of retirement age depends on the specific institutional structures of earnings, private pensions, and Social Security. The approach is a fruitful one, demonstrated by the robustness of our results across models and data sets. The consistency of our findings should make this book a useful guide to those who analyze and those who implement labor market policy.

I Thinking about Retirement in an Economic Context

Part I develops an economic model of retirement with four key features.

First, for most workers, retirement is a matter of choice. Certainly some people become too ill to continue working or are forced to retire on reaching a predetermined age of mandatory retirement. But forced retirement is the exception rather than the rule. Most workers retire before they need to.

Second, the variable of greatest interest is years of work, not hours. Retirement is a discrete choice and should be thought of in such terms. Most workers do not smoothly wind down hours and/or effort. Rather the prevalent pattern among older workers is to work full time until some cutoff date, which we call the age of retirement, and not work at all after that.

Third, economic factors have an important role to play in the retirement decision. Some people retire when they first can afford to. Others make careful comparisons of the income they would get from Social Security and private pensions if they retire versus the income they would earn if they went on working. To both types of individuals, economic factors matter a great deal.

Fourth, the retirement decision is best understood in an intertemporal (or life-cycle) framework. This means that people consider not only the income and leisure opportunities available to them if they retire this year but consider also the costs and benefits of waiting to retire. Examples are persons who plan to work several more years until meeting the minimum service requirement for a company pension or until reaching age 62, the age of first eligibility for Social Security benefits.

1 Determinants of Retirement

In this chapter we discuss the concept of retirement. We note ambiguities of classification and present definitions used in the empirical work that follows. Next, we review evidence on work and retirement patterns of the elderly. This evidence shows that regardless of how retirement is defined, older people on average are working less and retiring earlier. Third, we address the controversy between those who view retirement as a matter of choice and those who do not. Our evidence supports the choice view, a position we maintain in the balance of this book.

1. Defining Retirement

Retirement seems like an easy enough concept to define. Take the following example. Suppose that at age 65 you leave your lifelong job, accept an employer-provided pension, begin to collect Social Security benefits, leave the labor force, and depart for a life of sunshine and tranquillity on a Caribbean island. Everyone would agree that you had retired at that age.

Other cases are less clear-cut. Suppose you leave your lifelong employer at age 61 with a year's terminal sabbatical. Starting at age 62, you become eligible for a private pension from your employer's pension fund, which you accept. At age 65 you file for Social Security. You continue to earn a few thousand dollars a year as a part-time consultant to businesses and government agencies that wish to take advantage of your expertise. Have you retired? If so, at what age did you retire?

Different people might give different answers. One answer is a subjective self-assessment. We might ask you whether you are retired and classify you as such if you answer "Yes." Alternatively more objective measures might be used. One criterion is labor force participation. By that criterion the fact that you had worked continuously as a part-time consultant would lead to the classification "not retired," even if you viewed yourself otherwise. Other views might depend on whose perspective is taken: your employer probably would regard you as a retiree when you leave your job (age 61), the pension fund when it begins sending you pension checks (age 62), and the Social Security system when you first file for Social Security benefits (age 65).

Retirement is thus an ambiguous concept. Many definitions of retirement have been used by economists and other social scientists, including the following:

1. Subjective definition: You are retired if you answer affirmatively to a question such as "Are you retired?"

2. Labor force participation definition: You are retired when you cease participating in the labor force, that is, you completely stop working or looking for work.

3. Reduced effort definition: You are retired when your hours of work or your pay per hour fall below some fraction of their prior levels (say, one-half).

4. Leaving-the-main-employer definition: You are retired if you left a long-term job, even if you continue to work afterward at some postretirement job.

5. Private pension definition: You are classified as a retiree when you start receiving an employer-provided pension.

6. Social Security definition: You are classified as a retiree when you file for and receive Social Security benefits.

Empirical researchers typically choose one such definition and use it throughout their studies, though some (Gustafson, 1982; Gustman and Steinmeier, 1984) have compared alternative retirement measures in their empirical work. In this study we follow prevailing practice and use one specific definition of retirement for each data set employed. These data sets will be described in detail, but here we sketch only their most important features.

One data set is the Benefit Amounts Survey (BAS). The BAS gathered data from individual pension plans. Pension plans regard an individual as a retiree when he or she becomes a pension recipient. Consequently in our analysis using the BAS, the age of retirement is defined as the age of pension recipiency.

The other data set we use is the Longitudinal Retirement History Survey (LRHS), a panel study of households begun in 1969 and carried through until 1979. Respondents who were working in 1969 were asked to identify their employers. Given the ages of workers in our sample (in their late fifties in 1969), we interpret the 1969 employer as the main employer. In subsequent waves of the survey, respondents were asked whether they were still working

Table 1.1
Labor force participation rates by sex and age

Year	Males		Females	
	55–64	65+	55–64	65+
1955	87.9%	39.6%	32.5%	10.6%
1960	86.8	33.1	37.2	10.8
1965	84.6	27.9	41.1	10.0
1970	83.0	26.8	43.0	9.7
1975	75.6	21.6	40.9	8.2
1981	70.6	18.4	41.4	8.0

Source: *Employment and Training Report of the President* (1982), table A-5.

for the main employer; whether they were working for some other employer, and if so when they had moved; or whether they had left the labor force entirely, and if so when. In our analysis using the LRHS, the age of retirement is defined as the age at which an individual left his main employer.

2. Work and Retirement Patterns of the Elderly

Two facts about retirement patterns stand out: older people are retiring earlier and earlier through time and more people choose to retire at ages 62 and 65 than at adjacent ages.

For evidence on the trend to earlier retirement, we must rely on indirect measures since no time series on retirement ages is available. Two such proxies are the labor force attachment rates of older individuals and the age of Social Security acceptance. The data in table 1.1 indicate a well-known fact: male participation rates fell sharply over the last twenty-five years. In fact the rate of labor force participation for men in the 65+ age bracket fell by more than half. Among women the picture is different. The labor force participation rate of women aged 55 through 64 rose from 1955 to 1970, and since has fallen, whereas for men, labor force participation rates declined smoothly over the entire period. The rate of participation fell for women age 65+, but it fell for women less than it did for men. Overall the labor force participation evidence shows that men are retiring earlier; women too have been retiring earlier, at least since 1970 and maybe before that.

Another commonly used proxy for retirement patterns is the age of Social Security acceptance. Since the passage of the Social Security Act in 1935, the Social Security system has regarded age 65 as the normal age of retirement. For the last two decades workers of both sexes have been able to file for reduced

Table 1.2
Proportion of Social Security Beneficiaries accepting benefits with reduction for early retirement

Year	Proportion of Males	Proportion of Females
1961	4.7%	37.4%
1966	24.0	50.1
1971	38.6	60.3
1975	48.7	66.0
1982 (March)	57.9	70.2

Sources: Bixby (1976); Social Security Administration, *Social Security Bulletin* (1982), table Q-5.

Social Security benefits commencing as early as age 62. Table 1.2 shows the proportion of retirees accepting early Social Security benefits as opposed to normal benefits; the fraction of early retirees has risen steadily and rapidly for both sexes. Today the majority of both men and women start collecting Social Security before they turn 65. By this Social Security acceptance definition of retirement, men and women are retiring earlier.

The other feature of retirement ages worth noting is the specific distribution of retirement ages. Table 1.3 presents data for the BAS sample. It shows that more people retire at age 62 than at 61 or 63 and that more retire at 65 than at 64 or 66.[1]

Observers of these retirement patterns agree on the facts; disagreement arises over their interpretation. Some observers hold that retirement is compelled by such factors as poor health or mandatory retirement. Others maintain that retirement entails a choice based on balancing the monetary gains from continued work versus leisure forgone.

We see the evidence as supporting the choice view. The balance of this chapter defends this position.

3. The Role of Mandatory Retirement

There would be little point in analyzing retirement as a choice made by workers if most workers' choices were constrained by mandatory retirement provisions. But in fact, though workers in some industries face mandatory retirement at some age, the importance of mandatory retirement provisions is quite limited in the United States.

Studies have shown, contrary to popular opinion, that only a minority of workers are employed in jobs with mandatory retirement provisions. The

Table 1.3
Retirement ages in BAS sample

Age	Percentage of BAS Sample Retiring at That Age
60	10.7%
61	10.2
62	19.7
63	15.1
64	7.5
65	25.5
66	7.8
67	1.6
68	2.0

Source: BAS data file.

highest incidence of mandatory retirement was reported by Halpern (1978), who found that nearly half of male wage earners worked in jobs with mandatory retirement. Her conclusions were based on data from the National Longitudinal Survey for 1971. A lower figure—37 percent of all wage earners and 41 percent of male wage earners—was reported by Clark, Barker, and Cantrell (1979) for LRHS workers in 1971. Similarly Burkhauser and Quinn (1980) found that 37 percent of workers of both sexes were subject to mandatory retirement rules. These findings were also based on the LRHS, though for the period 1969 through 1975.

These percentages indicate that in the early 1970s only a minority of workers were employed in jobs that imposed mandatory retirement. But since many of these workers would have voluntarily retired before reaching the mandatory retirement age, the actual percentage attaining the age of mandatory retirement in their firms and forced to retire was considerably smaller. For instance, in our study of 390 workers in a major manufacturing firm with mandatory retirement at age 68 (Fields and Mitchell, 1984), we found that only 2 percent stayed on the job until the mandatory retirement age. Parnes and Nestel (Parnes, 1981) found that 5 percent of retirees were forced out by mandatory retirement, a conclusion drawn from the National Longitudinal Survey for 1976.

In 1978 an important institutional change circumscribed the role of mandatory retirement further. In that year an amendment to the Age Discrimination in Employment Act (ADEA) raised the allowable mandatory retirement age from 65 to 70 in most occupations. Very few workers remain at their jobs until age 70. For the sample of LRHS workers described in this book, the average retirement age was 63.9; only 9 percent remained with the employer as late as age 68. Some states have gone beyond the ADEA and have outlawed mandatory retirement altogether.

We thus conclude that the proportion of workers who retire because of mandatory retirement is quite small—perhaps 2 to 3 percent of the labor force and perhaps less. For most workers, the explanation for retirement patterns lies elsewhere.

4. The Role of Health

Another factor compelling workers to retire may be poor health. Many studies have concluded that poor health contributes to earlier retirement. These studies are of two kinds: survey evidence and revealed behavior. When people are asked why they retired, poor health is a common response. This is especially true among retirees who retire at a relatively young age. Clark and Spengler (1980) summarize earlier survey evidence. For instance, the National Longitudinal Survey found that 85 percent of white males aged 50 through 59 who were not in the labor force claimed that poor health limited the amount of work they could do or prevented them from working entirely (Parnes et al., 1974). At older ages the proportions retiring for health reasons diminish. Bixby (1976), for instance, found the following pattern in the Survey of Newly Entitled Beneficiaries: the percentage reporting poor health as the main reason for leaving their last job was 57 percent at age 62, 48 percent at ages 63–64, and 21 percent at age 65.

Survey evidence is also available from the LRHS. We have a sample of 1,103 white married men whose retirement ages and stated reasons for retirement could be ascertained. Let us define early retirement as leaving one's main job before reaching the age of 65. By this definition 539 (48.9 percent) of the men in our sample would be classified as early retirees. These 539 early retirees gave a variety of reasons for their retirement decision. Poor health was given by 132 (24.5 percent of the early retirees, 12.0 percent of the entire sample). Thus health is given as the reason for retirement by a substantial proportion of retirees.

How much credence to give to survey responses like these is debatable. Self-assessment measures are problematic for at least two reasons. One is that older people apparently find it much more socially acceptable to say that they retired because their health was poor than because they got tired of working. Another consideration is that many income-maintenance programs require that the applicant be certified as being in poor health. People may declare themselves to be in poor health in order to receive disability insurance or other welfare payments.[2] Thus people may report poor health as an ex post rationalization to hide their true reasons for retiring. This possibility has been discussed by a number of authors, including Parsons (1982, p. 81): "The declaration of poor health is, therefore, an economic phenomenon, one that makes difficult the estimation of the responsiveness of adult labor supply to economic incentives."

In the light of these difficulties, most economists have preferred to examine revealed behavior. To determine why people retire when they do and particularly the role poor health plays in retirement decisions, we can compare retirement patterns of older workers whose health is rated good with those whose health is rated poor.[3] When health measures have been included as explanatory variables in correlation or regression studies, the results of the vast majority of studies show that poor health is in fact associated with earlier retirement (Quinn, 1975, 1977; Reimers, 1977; Boskin and Hurd, 1978; Cullinan, 1979; Gordon and Blinder, 1980; Clark and Johnson, 1980; Parsons, 1982; Gustafson, 1982; Anderson and Burkhauser, 1983; Bazzoli, 1983), though a couple of studies (Burkhauser, 1976, 1979; Boskin, 1977) have not discerned such an effect. These results need to be interpreted with caution, however. Because health is a statistically significant determinant of retirement age does not mean that it is a dominant cause of retirement for most people. For older people in good health at the time of retirement, the explanation of retirement behavior lies elsewhere.

Finally, poor health can hardly explain the tendency toward earlier retirement over time. If any change in the health of the American population has taken place, it is in the direction of better health, not worse.[4] The effect should be later retirement, not earlier.

We conclude that poor health is the cause of retirement for a minority of the labor force. For the majority, however, retirement has other causes.

5. The Role of Social Security

The Social Security system in the United States is officially known as the Old Age and Survivors, Disability, and Health Insurance system. Our concern here is with the Old Age and Survivors Insurance program of Social Security, generally referred to as Social Security. (Disability insurance is referred to by that name, health insurance by Medicare.) We follow common usage throughout this book.

Since its inception in 1935, Social Security has grown to be the largest

Table 1.4
Growth in Social Security benefits over time

Year	Nominal Benefits		Consumer Price Index (1967 = 100) (3)	Real Benefits, in 1967 Dollars: (1 + 2) ÷ (3) (4)
	Average Retired Worker's Benefit (1)	Average Spouse's Benefit (2)		
1940	$ 22.60	$ 12.13	42.0	82.7
1945	24.19	12.82	53.9	68.7
1950	43.86	23.60	72.1	93.6
1955	61.90	33.07	80.2	118.4
1960	74.04	38.72	88.7	127.1
1965	83.92	43.63	94.5	135.0
1970	118.10	61.19	116.3	154.2
1975	207.18	105.19	161.2	193.4
1980	341.41	171.95	247.0	207.8
1983 (July)	422.80	215.27	298.2	214.0

Source: *Social Security Bulletin*, various issues.

domestic program in the United States. Thirty-six million Americans (virtually all of the elderly) receive Social Security checks each month. These checks totaled $162 billion in 1983, more than all other income-transfer programs combined.

The following features will help us determine Social Security's effects on retirement:

Growth of Coverage The Social Security system originally covered only a small fraction of the working population. Additional occupations were included over time. Today nearly all jobs and all workers (more than 90 percent) are covered by Social Security. The largest group of uncovered workers is federal government employees, but beginning in 1984 all newly hired federal government workers must join Social Security. The only significant remaining groups of workers left uncovered by Social Security are some state and local government workers whose employers voluntarily opted out of Social Security and federal government workers hired before 1984.

Growth of Benefits Social Security benefits have increased in generosity over the years (see table 1.4). The average retired worker received a monthly benefit of $423 in 1983, nearly twenty times the nominal benefit in 1940. Inflation reduces the value of the increase, of course, but even after correcting for inflation, the real benefit of a Social Security recipient is more than three times that of a beneficiary in 1945. In addition Social Security benefits have grown relative to earnings. A commonly used measure is the Social Security replacement rate, that is, the ratio of Social Security benefits to preretirement earnings. The Social Security replacement rate for a worker with average earnings at age 65 increased from 19 percent in 1950 to 51 percent in 1980 (Munnell, 1977).

Indexation of Benefits Social Security benefits are well protected against inflation. Until 1979 benefits increased faster than the rate of inflation due to inadvertent double indexation from 1972 to 1979 and generous increases before that. Now, though, benefits rise in proportion to the consumer price index. The full indexation of Social Security benefits has led a number of economists (for example, Hurd and Shoven, 1983) to the conclusion that the elderly as a group are well protected against inflation—much better protected, they argue, than the nonelderly population.

Generosity of Benefits The average worker's benefit, combined with the average spouse's benefit, was $638 per month in 1983, 25 percent more than the official U.S. poverty line for an elderly, nonfarm family of two. The maximum benefit is considerably higher than that. Take, for instance, a worker who earned at least the Social Security taxable maximum.[5] The worker and spouse together would qualify for Social Security benefits of $1,063 per month if they are both 65 years old in 1983—67 percent more than average and more than twice the poverty line.

Supplemental Security Income The elderly with very low incomes can receive additional benefits beyond their entitlements from the Old Age and Survivors Insurance program of Social Security. This program, known as Supplemental Security Income (SSI), provides benefits to low-income elderly, the blind, and the disabled. To quality for the elderly program, an individual must be 65 or over. Only limited earnings, unearned income, and assets are permitted. Over 1.5 million aged recipients received SSI payments in 1983, averaging $407 per month.

The Importance of Social Security Income Social Security is now the single most important source of income for the elderly.[6] Table 1.5 shows that more of the elderly receive income from Social Security than from any other source. Fifty-nine percent of the elderly households rely on Social Security for 50 percent or more of total income. Social Security provides 40 percent of aggregate income for the elderly, as compared with 22 percent provided by assets, 19 percent due to earnings, and 14 percent from employer-provided pensions. Social Security income is particularly important for the low-income elderly, as shown in table 1.6.

Table 1.5
Fraction of aged household units receiving some income from various sources, 1980

Source	Percentage
Social Security	90
Assets	66
Employer-provided pension	34
Earnings	23
Public assistance	10

Source: Upp (1983).

Table 1.6
Importance of Social Security as an income source for the elderly, by household income level, 1980

Household Income	Percentage of Households Receiving More Than One-Third of Their Income from Social Security
Under $5,000	89
$5,000–9,999	73
$10,000–19,999	33
$20,000 and over	1

Source: Upp (1983).

Age of Eligibility At age 65, covered workers can collect normal Social Security benefits; however, they are eligible to collect reduced benefits as early as age 62. As we saw in table 1.2, the majority of Social Security recipients accept reduced benefits before reaching age 65; moreover the percentage accepting reduced benefits has increased steadily over time. Recent changes in the law will increase the age of eligibility for normal benefits to age 66 in 2009 and age 67 in 2027. Reduced benefits, however, will continue to be available beginning at age 62.

From these facts, we conclude that Social Security facilitates retirement choices. Older persons are able to draw substantial retirement incomes beginning as early as age 62. Social Security compels workers' retirement choices only to the extent that they might retire even earlier if they could collect reduced benefits at a younger age. Indeed the age 62 minimum is probably the most important reason that retirement ages cluster age 62, as observed in table 1.3. Nothing in Social Security forces workers to retire before they want to.

6. The Role of Private Pensions

Nine million Americans—one-third of all elderly households—receive private pensions.[7] Since over 90 percent of elderly households receive Social Security benefits, private pensions are numerically much less important than is Social Security. This difference is reflected in a comparison of income shares: private pensions account for some 14 to 16 percent of total income of the elderly (Kotlikoff and Smith, 1983; Upp, 1983) whereas Social Security accounts for about 40 percent; however, the dollar amounts per recipient are much more alike. Data presented in chapter 3 show that private pension income for those who receive pensions about equals the Social Security benefit received by an unmarried worker.

Private pensions have been growing rapidly since 1950.[8] Between 1950 and 1980 the percentage of payroll going to pensions increased from 1 percent to 6 percent. Thirty-seven percent of workers today are employed in jobs where they are covered by private pensions; in 1950 the percentage was 19 percent.

Private pensions enable workers to retire earlier because most pension plans have provisions for early retirement. In some plans workers are eligible for pensions after completing a specified period of service, in others on reaching a specified age, and in still others when age plus years of service reaches some critical value. The availability of such retirement income, often commencing before the worker can start to collect Social Security benefits (age 62), facilitates retirement choices. Pensions do not compel workers to retire; they permit them to, if they choose.

One matter of some controversy is whether private pensions are structured so as to tilt the retirement choice one way or the other. Pension plans sometimes give a sizable bonus for continued work; for instance, a worker is often offered a pension to stay with the firm for a specified time, say ten years. This creates an incentive for the worker not to retire in the eighth or ninth year on the job. On the other hand, pension plans often do the opposite, reducing the total pension if retirement is deferred. For example, the United Auto Workers pension plan offers eligible workers very large pension benefits if they retire before age 62. The workers lose these benefits if they remain on the job, a powerful incentive toward earlier retirement.

7. The Role of Assets

Sixty-six percent of aged households receive some income from assets other than private pension and Social Security wealth. This compares to 90 percent who receive some income from Social Security and 34 percent who receive

Table 1.7
Asset income as a proportion of total cash income of the elderly, by income class, 1979

Cash Income in 1979	Income from Assets
Less than $5,000	6%
$5,000–9,999	15
$10,000–14,999	19
$15,000–24,999	22
$25,000 and over	27
All elderly	20

Source: EBRI (1982), table I-20.

some income from employer-provided pensions. One should not jump to the conclusion that asset income is the second most important source of income for most elderly households, however. Several factors suggest otherwise.

One is that asset income is distributed very unequally. The Employee Benefit Research Institute (EBRI, 1982) reported that mean asset income is five and a half times the median, a clear indication of skewness.

A second factor is that assets are held in largely illiquid form. Friedman and Sjogren (1981) examined the assets of the elderly as they retired. They found that the median value of assets for families with assets was $33,100 in 1979; however, the most important asset was home equity, the median value of which was $27,000 among households with home equity. Reverse mortgages notwithstanding, home equity is one of the most illiquid of assets. Seventy-five percent of families with assets held life insurance policies and annuities, also illiquid. By contrast, the median value of liquid assets (bank accounts and stocks and bonds, for example) was just $7,300. The income that could be derived from such assets is very small—well under $1,000 per year even when interest rates are very high.

Asset income is also received disproportionately by the well-to-do. On average, income from assets accounts for 20 percent of total income of the elderly; however, asset income as a percentage of total income rises as we move up the income scale (table 1.7).

Finally, these asset income figures impute income values to home equities, annuities, life insurance policies, and other illiquid assets. At least 80 percent of assets of the elderly are illiquid. Therefore asset income received in cash can amount to no more than about 5 percent of the total incomes of the elderly.

In sum, cash income from assets is a minor source of income for most of the elderly population.

8. The Relative Importance of Economic Factors and Health

The evidence that most workers chose when to retire and that economic factors played an important role in this decision raises the question, Which is the more important determinant of retirement age, economic factors or health? An answer cannot be found readily in the literature because past researchers have reported regression coefficients and t-statistics but not the proportions of variance associated with sets of variables. To fill this gap, we report briefly on the results of an analysis of variance (ANOVA).

The data set used in the ANOVA calculation, the empirical specification of the economic and health variables, and the specific numerical results appear in chapter 5. (The ANOVA calculations will make sense only after we have described the modeling strategy, data set, variable construction, and other details, which follow in chapters 2 through 5.) For now let consider just the results.

Six alternative specifications were formulated; all yielded essentially the same results: of the variation in retirement ages that can be explained, economic variables explain about three-quarters and health about one-quarter. In short, economic variables explain most of what can be explained. The view of retirement as one of choice receives additional confirmation.

9. Summary

This chapter has presented evidence showing that economic factors are of preeminent importance in determining older workers' retirement behavior. Health and other noneconomic factors matter too, but they matter less. More workers have better retirement income opportunities available to them than ever before. These enhanced income opportunities enable people to retire earlier. Older workers have not been forced to retire earlier; they have chosen to. The remainder of this book explores precisely how economic factors matter in the retirement decision.

2 The Retirement Decision in an Intertemporal Framework

1. Introduction to the Age-of-Retirement Model

In this chapter we develop a structural age-of-retirement model in a life-cycle context. The model aims to capture the essential features of the retirement decision and guides the empirical work in the remainder of this book. This analysis is based on the theoretical work of Burbidge and Robb (1980), MacDonald and Carliner (1980), Crawford and Lilien (1981), and Fields and Mitchell (1981).[1]

The age-of-retirement model has five highlights:

1. The decision is intertemporal. The individual must decide how long to work this year, how long to work next year, and so on up to the end of his or her planning horizon.

2. The decision is how many years to work before retiring. Each period's decision is dichotomous: to work or not.

3. The goal is to choose that retirement age which maximizes intertemporal utility. Utility is assumed to depend positively on consumption of goods and years of leisure.

4. The choice is constrained by economic opportunities. Earnings, private pensions, and Social Security enter explicitly into the retirement decision.

5. The retirement decision is affected by economic opportunities at all dates—past, present, and future. Knowledge of current economic opportunities alone is insufficient.

Models with other features might be built instead. Take, for instance, the specification of hours of work. Our age-of-retirement model assumes that the optimal pattern is to work full time and then retire. Most individuals seem to regard this as the optimal pattern, but other patterns are possible. Figure 2.1 illustrates some of the possibilities. Each vertical axis measures the fraction of

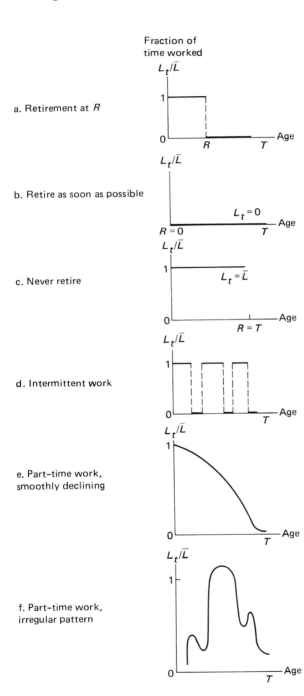

Figure 2.1
Alternative retirement patterns

time worked in period t, where L_t is number of hours worked and $\bar{L}$ is total available work time. Figure 2.1a illustrates full work followed by full retirement. Other plans might be optimal for other people. For instance, some individuals may retire as soon as possible, as illustrated in figure 2.1b. At the other extreme, some might prefer never to retire, choosing instead to leave their pension accruals to their heirs (figure 2.1c). Another possibility is intermittent work, as shown in figure 2.1d. Other arrangements might include part-time employment declining smoothly with age (figure 2.1e) or changing irregularly with age (figure 2.1f).

The theoretical work in this chapter does not allow for variable hours of work or intermittent work periods. One reason for this decision is to focus attention on the key aspects of the retirement decision: how budget sets and preferences affect older workers' retirement choices. The age-of-retirement model permits statements such as "ceteris paribus, workers who have higher retirement incomes at the time of the retirement decision will tend to retire earlier" or "given the choice between any two retirement ages, workers who stand to gain a larger pension increase by continuing to work will tend to retire later, ceteris paribus." Models other than the age-of-retirement model have proved less tractable in generating insights like these.[2] The age-of-retirement focus is also interesting for policy purposes, where the goal is to predict how changes in income variables would alter average retirement ages.

Turning our attention from theoretical formulations to empirical specifications, the dependent variable could be any of several different measures: hours of work per year, the probability of retiring at an early age rather than at some normal age, the probability of working full time at some date or age, or the age of retirement. Previous researchers have tended to focus on cross-sectional probabilities of older workers' being in a particular labor force status at the time of the survey. Our empirical work, presented in part III of this book and in companion work (Fields and Mitchell, 1984; Mitchell and Fields, 1983, 1984), is the first to take the age of retirement as the dependent variable.

Irrespective of the choice of dependent variable, the explanatory variables for a life-cycle analysis of retirement must include measures of economic and noneconomic conditions at all relevant dates—past, present, and future. To include the present is obvious. One's current work or retirement status clearly depends on one's current economic opportunities, health, and other conditions. The past influences current conditions and decisions by affecting both measurable current attributes (for example, earnings today reflect past investment in human capital) and nonmeasurable current attributes (such as individual-specific preferences for work versus leisure). The future enters into current decisions because what one does today depends on the future consequences of one's actions; for example, if I receive a pension after working five years for my employer but I have thus far only worked four, the availability of a pension after another year's work presumably would influence my decision to remain with my present firm one more year or retire or take a job elsewhere.

To sum up the discussion, we have the following functional relationship:

$$R = f(X_{t-}, X_t, X_{t+}),\tag{2.1}$$

where R is some measure of retirement status and X_{t-}, X_t, and X_{t+} are measures of economic and noneconomic conditions in the past, present, and future, respectively.

Despite the clear theoretical appeal of this approach to theoretical modeling, most empirical researchers have used only current values of explanatory variables rather than the more appropriate streams over the individual's remaining lifetime.[3] The empirical research described here is the first analysis that explicitly derives for each worker in the sample under study an intertemporal budget set for all possible retirement ages. Other researchers usually have had less complete data files and generally were able to do no more than include the change in present discounted value of pension income and/or Social Security benefits if retirement is postponed from the date of the survey until some arbitrary date, usually the following year.

The present analysis is also unique in combining data on all of the components of the intertemporal budget set—earnings, private pension, and Social Security benefits—constructing present discounted values of expected future income from all these sources.

Finally, a word is in order on how the age-of-retirement model relates to the notion of implicit contracts. It is now widely agreed that pensions are part of an implicit contract between workers and firms (Lazear, 1979, 1983; Ippolito, 1983). This view posits that the firm implicitly agrees to employ a worker until that worker voluntarily agrees to leave. The worker in turn implicitly agrees to be suitably productive on the job. In any given year the worker's productivity may differ from his or her pay. It may be optimal in some circumstances for the firm to pay the worker less than the value of his or her marginal product when the worker is young and more than the marginal product when the worker is old. The contract then specifies a final period in which the firm pays the worker a pension even though the worker has retired and is not producing anything at all. The pension serves as a kind of bond ensuring the implicit contract; workers are induced to work harder during their working years and not to shirk on the job.

Implicit contract models allow the firm to set up incentives for workers to make choices in ways that the firm finds desirable. For example, a firm in which productivity falls off as workers age may find it advantageous to tilt its pension structure so that pensions are highest when the worker retires earliest. The tilt is intended to induce workers to choose to retire earlier.

The age-of-retirement model is designed to capture this notion. Age-of-retirement models and implicit contract models are not competing; they are integrally related. The theoretical presumption is that workers' choices at least partially reflect the incentives put before them. At issue are two questions: how prevalent are such incentives, and how responsive are workers to them? These are empirical questions for which evidence is offered below.

2. Budget Sets and Preferences

In the age-of-retirement model, as in other economic contexts, the basic building blocks of the choice process are budget sets and preferences. The intertemporal budget set is the amount of income that an individual would receive from earnings, private pensions, and Social Security for each alternative retirement age. Conditioning the retirement decision are the individual's preferences for the income gained from continued work compared to the extra leisure enjoyed by retiring earlier. For purposes of the theoretical discussion, both the intertemporal utility function and the intertemporal budget set are viewed as stationary over time. In postulating that retirement choices depend on budget sets and preferences, we do not mean to imply that financial factors are the only considerations that affect retirement behavior. Health, occupation, family situation, and many other factors matter as well. The way we allow for these other factors is through the older worker's preferences and/or income opportunities.

The construction of the budget set is illustrated with the aid of figure 2.2. Let us take age 60 as the starting point for retirement planning; call this date zero. Regard the individual's planning horizon as T years long, though in fact he or she might die before then. Each year the individual continues to work, he or she receives E_t earnings after taxes and pension contributions, if any. The worker who retires at an intermediate date such as I receives P_t in retirement income from private pension (PP) and Social Security (SS). Ordinarily retirement income replaces only a fraction of previous earnings, so $P_t < E_t$. P_t is a positive function of the age of retirement (R) and the year in question (t). P_t increases with R because private pension plans and Social Security ordinarily provide higher annual retirement benefits to workers who defer retirement. P_t increases with t because Social Security and some private pensions award postretirement increases as an offset to inflation. Of course, if

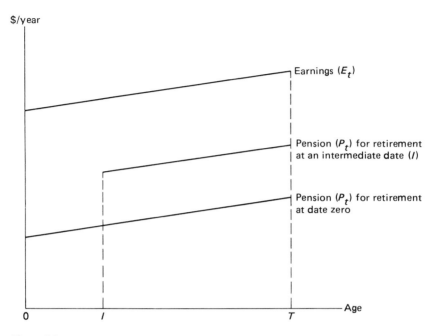

Figure 2.2
Annual values of earnings and pensions

retirement is postponed, the higher annual pension is received for fewer years.

To compare streams of incomes received over time, it is necessary to construct present discounted values and sum the various amounts. The present discounted value of expected income (PDVY) for retirement at age R is given by

$$PDVY = \int_{t=0}^{R} E_t \delta_t dt + \int_{R}^{T} (PP_t + SS_t)\delta_t dt, \tag{2.2}$$

where the E_t are the earnings in the working years from O to R, PP_t and SS_t are, respectively, the private pension and Social Security benefits in the retirement years from R to T, and δ_t is a discount factor reflecting time preference and mortality. To find the monetary value of working the Rth year, differentiate (2.2) to obtain:

$$\frac{\partial PDVY}{\partial R} = \underbrace{E_R \delta_R}_{(a)} + \underbrace{\frac{\partial \left[\int_{R+1}^{T} (PP_t + SS_t)\delta_t dt \right]}{\partial R}}_{(b)} - \underbrace{(PP_R + SS_R)\delta_R.}_{(c)} \tag{2.3}$$

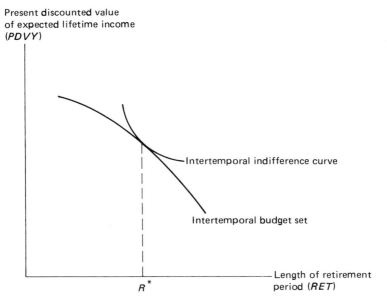

Figure 2.3
Intertemporal budget set and preferences as determinants of the optimal retirement age

The right-hand side of equation (2.3) consists of three terms: (a) earnings in year R, plus (b) accrual of future private pension and Social Security benefits by working in year R, minus (c) private pension and Social Security benefits forgone in year R if the individual works in that year. Ordinarily pension accrual (term b) is nonnegative[4] and earnings (term a) exceed pensions (term c).[5] Under these conditions, PDVY is an increasing function of retirement age R, or, alternatively, a decreasing function of length of the retirement period RET. Such a pattern is illustrated by the intertemporal budget set in figure 2.3.

Preferences are represented by an intertemporal utility function. Utility is presumed to be a positive function of two factors—planned lifetime consumption (C) and leisure during the retirement period (RET)—and to be concave in both arguments:

$$U_i = U(C_i, RET_i), \quad U(\ ) \text{ concave.} \tag{2.4}$$

Lifetime consumption (C) is planned to equal the present discounted value of income over the remainder of the individual's life (PDVY), plus wealth as of the time of the retirement decision (W_0), minus bequests at the time of the retirement decision (B_0):

$$C = PDVY + W_0 - B_0. \tag{2.5}$$

An individual with such a utility function would work longer if by so doing he or she gains enough extra income to compensate for loss of leisure.[6] The rate at which he or she is willing to trade off income for leisure and retain the same level of utility is illustrated in the indifference map in figure 2.3.

3. The Optimal Retirement Age

The optimal retirement age in this age-of-retirement model is that which maximizes intertemporal utility (2.4) subject to the intertemporal budget set (2.2).[7] This is the point labeled R^* in figure 2.3. At this point the individual is on the highest indifference curve consistent with his or her feasible budget set. The marginal utility of consumption from an extra year's work is equated to the marginal utility of an additional year of leisure. More formally, the first-order condition is

$$\frac{\partial U_i}{\partial C_i} \frac{\partial PDVY_i}{\partial R_i} = \frac{\partial U_i}{\partial RET_i} \tag{2.6}$$

for retirement in the interior of the interval $(0, T)$ to be optimal;[8] if this cannot be satisfied by an equality—for example, if

$$\frac{\partial U_i}{\partial C_i} \frac{\partial PDVY_i}{\partial R_i} < \frac{\partial U_i}{\partial RET_i} \quad \text{for all } R_i \tag{2.7}$$

—then the optimum is to retire immediately.

It is instructive to ask how the optimal retirement age responds to changes in the budget set. Theory reveals surprisingly few unambiguous results. First, higher earnings may result in earlier or later retirement because offsetting substitution and income effects are set into motion. When earnings are higher, the individual forgoes more money by retiring earlier; this substitution effect by itself creates an incentive for prolonged work. Reasoning just this far, many authors have maintained that higher earnings will result in later retirement. This conclusion is correct if and only if the worker faces a dichotomous choice: work one more period or retire now. Faced with such a choice, the worker confronts only a substitution effect by which higher earnings lead to later retirement. But in a multiperiod context, another effect is also set into motion: an income effect. After the individual has worked for a time at the higher earnings level, he or she is richer. One of the ways to spend this additional wealth is to buy more leisure. If leisure is a normal good, this income effect by itself leads in the direction of earlier retirement when earnings rise. Hence the substitution effect and income effect work in the opposing directions—the substitution effect inducing later retirement in response to an earnings increase, the income effect inducing earlier retirement. Economic theory is thus ambiguous, and which effect dominates becomes an empirical question.

Second, a higher rate of pension accrual may result in earlier or later retirement. The rate of pension accrual is the amount by which private pension and/or Social Security benefits increase if the individual goes on working. For example, in the case of a pension plan where pension benefit is a multiple of years of service, a higher multiple implies a higher pension accrual. A higher pension accrual has ambiguous effects on the optimal retirement age; once again the reason has to do with offsetting substitution and income effects. As with earnings, the substitution effect leads to later retirement because more is forgone if the individual retires early. In the case of a dichotomous choice (work one more period or do not), this is the end of the story. But in a multiperiod context, there is also an income effect because after the first period, the individual is wealthier and can buy more leisure with this extra income, thus retiring earlier. The ambiguous theoretical effect of higher pensions on retirement ages has been overlooked by many writers who assume that a higher pension should always produce earlier retirement. This arises in one special case, having to do not with pension accruals but with pension levels.

Third, a higher base pension holding constant the rate of pension accrual would result in earlier retirement. Such an increase in pension creates only an income effect in the direction of earlier retirement; the absence of an opposing substitution effect renders the result unambiguous.

More technically these comparative static results may be derived by substituting the change in the budget constraint (2.3) into the first-order condition (2.6) to obtain:

$$\frac{\partial U}{\partial C}(C, RET)\left[E_R\delta_R - P_R\delta_R + \int_{R+1}^{T} \frac{\partial P(t, R)}{\partial R}\delta_t dt\right] - \frac{\partial U}{\partial RET}(C, RET) = 0,$$
(2.8)

and then differentiating with respect to the parameter of interest. At the optimal retirement age, the individual equates the utility value of the Rth year's earnings and higher pension benefits in later years with the utility value of the loss of the Rth year's pension income and leisure. Results of the comparative static analysis are summarized in table 2.1, which shows the ambiguities of the earnings and pension accrual results and the unambiguous base pension result.

Table 2.1.
Comparative statics

Parameter Change	Effect of parameter change on:					
	Marginal Utility of Consumption, $\frac{\partial U}{\partial C}$	Earnings, E_{R_0}	Pension, P_{R_0}	Rate of Pension Accrual, $\frac{\partial P}{\partial R}$	Marginal Utility of Leisure, $\frac{\partial U}{\partial RET}$	Net Effect on Age of Retirement R^*
Higher earnings stream, holding pension accrual and base pension constant	+	+	+ or zero	+ or zero	+	Ambiguous
Higher pension accrual, holding earnings stream and base pension constant	−	zero	+	+	+	Ambiguous
Higher base pension, holding earnings stream and pension accrual constant	−	zero	+	zero	+	Earlier

Note: Evaluated at original optimum R_0.

4. Other Approaches

Some readers may wonder why we selected the modeling approach we did. This section briefly describes several of the possible alternatives and our reasons for not choosing them.

Reoptimization Consistent with virtually all other theoretical studies of the retirement decision, we develop the age-of-retirement model in a certainty framework. We are aware that such stochastic events as the possible onset of ill health and unanticipated inflation render the environment uncertain. Although retirement plans may change in response to such uncertain events, we have excluded them from our age-of-retirement model. To analyze these in a more comprehensive framework would require stochastic dynamic programming. A cost-benefit calculation of the expected payoff from adopting a probabilistic framework led us to consider only certainty models.[9] The decision to use a certainty framework puts us in the company of nearly all other retirement researchers, as well as others who have worked on such life-cycle choices as lifetime savings patterns, education investments, and child-bearing decisions, which also are inherently uncertain. But even if we wanted to build a probabilistic theoretical model (it seems completely out of the question even to think it feasible), the empirical model requires us to specify a private pension matrix with double subscripting. For example, assuming that the retirement decision is made at age 60, the entry $PP_{65,68}$ in the PP matrix is the pension that the individual thinks he or she will receive at age 68 by retiring at age 65, as viewed from the perspective of age 60. With reoptimization we would need triple subscripting—for example, what at age 60 he thinks he will receive at age 68 if he retires at age 65, what at age 61 he thinks he will receive at age 68 if he retires at age 65, and so on. Clearly this is outside the realm of empirical possibility at present.

Hazard Functions Unlike the reoptimization model, which is motivated primarily by theoretical considerations, a different modeling strategy arises from predominantly empirical concerns. This is hazard function modeling. Labor economists have come to be familiar with these models through work on duration of unemployment by Lancaster (1979), Tuma and Robins (1980), Kiefer and Neumann (1982), and Flinn and Heckman (1982). Hazard function models explain an intertemporal phenomenon (unemployment in each of a number of weeks) by both deterministic and stochastic components. The deterministic components include features of the individual or of the environment that affect the probability of leaving unemployment; these include such variables as age, sex, race, and geographic location. The stochastic component is a random variable, reflecting the fact that some people receive job offers while others, otherwise identical, do not.

Recent unpublished studies by Diamond and Hausman (1984) and Hausman and Wise (1983) have cast the retirement decision in a hazard function framework. The Diamond-Hausman model specifies that the probability of retiring in any given year is a function of age, health, demographic variables, and economic conditions in the year of the survey. The Hausman-Wise model includes the variables mentioned plus the increment to Social Security benefits if the individual were to wait another year to retire. The probabilistic feature allowing health to change from good to bad is central to their analysis. But what their model does not do, and what the life-cycle model is designed to achieve, is to build in the set of economic opportunities available to the potential retiree at all possible future retirement ages. The strength of the hazard function model is that it is fundamentally stochastic. Its weakness is that it is not yet able to handle a full life-cycle framework. It remains for econometricians to devise a comprehensive, well-formulated stochastic life-cycle empirical model. Until then empirical researchers must content themselves with having either a life-cycle model or a probabilistic model but not both. We have chosen the former in this study.

Reduced Form Estimation The theoretical model developed in this chapter and the empirical models that follow are structural in that the retirement decision is expressed as a function of the components of the intertemporal budget set and of preferences. A different empirical approach was adopted by Heckman and MaCurdy (1980). They estimated an intertemporal labor supply model in which all aspects of future economic opportunities were collapsed into a single fixed effect. By using such a variable, they were able to formulate a life-cycle labor supply model without having to know the formulas determining Social Security and private pension benefits for their sample of workers. This is both an advantage and a disadvantage. The advantage is that they were able to study the determinants of current labor supply in a full life-cycle context while possessing limited information. The disadvantage is that we cannot learn from their reduced form formulation how earnings opportunities, Social Security benefits, and private pension structures affect the retirement decision since all of these structural variables are absent. Because we are concerned with structural estimation, we did not avail ourselves of the Heckman-MaCurdy specification.

5. Summary

The retirement decision is best thought of in an intertemporal context. This implies that economic opportunities in the past, present, and future are needed to explain the choice of retirement date. This chapter models the retirement decision as a function of intertemporal preferences and an intertemporal budget set. Besides leisure, the streams of earnings, private pensions, and Social Security income for each alternative retirement age also enter into the analysis.

In the age-of-retirement framework, the optimal retirement date is that which equates the marginal utility of the extra earnings and pension accruals gained by working with the marginal disutility of forgone pension income and leisure. A higher earnings stream or a higher rate of pension accrual would have an ambiguous effect on the optimal age of retirement. An unambiguous effect is found only for higher base pension; other things equal, the higher the base pension, the earlier the optimal retirement age.

Other theoretical and empirical approaches might have been used instead. These others have advantages of their own—particularly allowance for random events—but also disadvantages: either they are empirically unimplementable, or they sacrifice the full life-cycle framework on which our analysis is based, or they do not provide structural estimates of parameters of interest. We opt for an empirically implementable, structural, life-cycle model.

II Income Opportunities for Older Workers

Part II develops and examines the intertemporal budget set facing older workers. The perspective adopted is that of a worker contemplating retirement at alternative ages. We ask two questions: (1) What income would a typical worker receive from earnings, private pension, and Social Security by retiring at age 60? (2) How would this worker's earnings, private pension, Social Security, and total income change by postponing retirement to age 61, 62, . . . , 68?

These questions are answered in two chapters. Chapter 3 describes the data bases and methodologies used to construct the intertemporal budget sets. It also presents results for two data sets, the Benefit Amounts Survey of the Department of Labor and the Longitudinal Retirement History Survey of the Social Security Administration. Chapter 4 uses the detailed private pension information from the Benefit Amounts Survey to explore similarities and differences in the way different pension plans reward continued work.

3   The Intertemporal Budget Sets in Two Data Bases

This chapter develops an empirical counterpart to the intertemporal budget set depicted theoretically in figure 2.3. Such information is of interest for two reasons. One is in determining the incentives for retirement. Some authors such as Lazear (1982) have suggested that firms structure their pension plans so that the present discounted value of pension benefits is greater the earlier the worker retires. Others such as Burkhauser and Turner (1981) maintain that Social Security creates similar incentives in the direction of early retirement. The second reason for focusing on the intertemporal budget set is that it is a central determinant of older workers' retirement decisions. In this chapter we summarize the microeconomic data used in the retirement analysis of part III.

We approach the intertemporal budget set from the point of view of a prospective retiree. Workers in our sample are assumed to be making their retirement decisions around the age of 60 in 1970. An individual's choice of retirement age is posited to depend on what he anticipated that income and leisure opportunities would be at alternative future retirement ages. It is extremely difficult to obtain data on all of these variables, and no one data set contains exactly what is needed.

In this book we use two different surveys, the Social Security Administration's Longitudinal Retirement History Survey (LRHS) and the Labor Department's Benefit Amounts Survey (BAS). The main advantage of the LRHS is its representativeness; its main disadvantage is its inaccuracy in gauging private pension amounts. By contrast the BAS offers full details on pension rules, but only for a limited number of pension plans. These and other features of the two data sets are described in this chapter.

1. The Data Bases

The Longitudinal Retirement History Survey

After reviewing the advantages and disadvantages of several candidate data sets, we concluded that the LRHS was relatively well suited for our purposes.[1] It was first fielded in 1969, and reinterviews took place at two-year intervals through 1979. Detailed information on work status, health and marital status, earnings, current pension and Social Security income, and expected future pension benefits was obtained for all sample members. From the group originally surveyed, we selected a sample size of 1,024 for the present study.

This LRHS sample consists of white married men with spouse present, age 59–61 in 1969, employed as private sector wage and salaried workers and not institutionalized over the survey period. These restrictions were imposed for the following reasons: choosing workers in a narrow age range was required in order to ensure that retirement patterns could be observed during the ensuing waves of the survey; it is a compromise between averting incomplete work lives on the one hand and mortality bias on the other. The sample was also limited to employees because the concept of retirement is poorly defined for the self-employed. The bedridden and seriously ill were excluded since economic incentives will most likely play a different role for this group than for others. Finally, we included only private sector workers because we lack data on pension levels for retirees from government jobs.

For this sample of workers, retirement is defined as the age at which each worker left his 1969 employment. This is computed by comparing each individual's job in later years with that held in the first year of the survey, 1969.

The Labor Department's Benefit Amounts Survey

Although the LRHS has several features that make it valuable to analysts of retirement patterns, it has one serious drawback: it does not report the rules determining pension benefits for workers covered by employer-provided plans. Thus we were required to impute potential pension amounts, which is the best that can be done with that data base but may be quite inaccurate.

For this reason we also employ a second data source, the BAS, which contains a great deal more information on workers' retirement incomes. In 1978 the Pensions and Welfare Benefits Program at the Labor Department selected a sample of private pension plans filing summary plan descriptions (SPDs) as required under the Employee Retirement Income Security Act of

1974. These SPDs contained extensive data on pension formulas used to determine retirement benefits for the workers in each plan. Every sample plan also provided data to the Labor Department on its pension recipients. These data included the birth year and the year of retirement of each pension recipient. The Social Security Administration then matched this employer-provided information with individual earnings history records and basic demographic information.

Establishing the exact benefit formulas for all defined benefit plans in the survey proved unexpectedly complicated; the data sample we use in estimation is therefore a subset of the overall file. Using the SPDs as well as union contracts and other sources, we constructed pension formulas for fourteen defined benefit pension plans.[2] Ten of these plans had enough data on retirees so they could be included in this chapter and in part III; the other four are used only in chapter 4, where retiree behavior is not required. We recognize that the BAS subsample of pension plans is small; clearly the findings we report must be viewed as exploratory rather than representative of the entire universe of workers with pensions. Still, ten or fourteen plans are better than one, which is all that was available to us before (Fields and Mitchell, 1984) or to Burkhauser (1979) or to Burtless and Hausman (1982). No larger data set containing information on both pensions and their beneficiaries is currently publicly available.

We also were compelled to impose additional restrictions in choosing our sample of workers. Defined benefit plans determine pension benefit amounts partly, and sometimes exclusively, on the basis of years of service; workers whose years of service could not be ascertained in the data file were therefore excluded. Workers were also dropped from the sample if their files lacked information on their Social Security earnings histories, needed for calculating Social Security benefits and for projecting earnings beyond the age of retirement. As in the case of the LRHS, we include in the BAS sample only those individuals who reached the age of mandatory retirement by the time of the survey in 1978. This is to minimize sample truncation due to self-selection. Therefore these data are free from "censored spells" problems. At the same time we wished to avoid mortality bias, so we selected the youngest possible group of workers in the sample—those born in 1909 and 1910. Finally, the BAS analysis includes only men. The reason for this limitation is that the BAS survey contains no information on spouse's work status; this omission is much more serious for women than for men.

The BAS data set thus consists of 8,733 males from ten firms with defined benefit pension plans, who retired between the ages of 60 and 68, and for whom complete data were available on retirement year, years of service, and Social Security earnings history.

Comparing the Data Sets

Both the LRHS and the BAS have most of the core economic variables needed for empirical analysis. Both contain Social Security earnings history records, from which earnings and Social Security benefits can be estimated. The LRHS sample is national in coverage, whereas the BAS sample we used is drawn from ten firms only. The LRHS contains information on marital status and health; the BAS does not. Offsetting the advantages of the LRHS is one critical disadvantage: the formulas determining workers' private pension benefits are not known. The BAS remedies this gap. Therefore the two data sets are complementary, the LRHS being more representative in coverage and containing information on marital status and health, the BAS providing a better indication of private pension benefits for a selected sample.

2. Constructing the Intertemporal Budget Sets

The LRHS

The income from earnings, private pension, and Social Security available at alternate retirement ages is necessary for empirical analysis of the retirement decision. This intertemporal budget set was constructed with laborious effort and calculation. The main features of each component follow.

Earnings Earnings imputations are based on Social Security earnings history data for each individual. However, since earnings are reported only up to the Social Security tax maximum in the relevant year, the earnings of workers who reached the tax ceiling would be understated if their Social Security earnings were taken to represent their total earnings. To allow for earnings in excess of ceiling, we modified an algorithm devised by Fox (1976), which uses information on quarters of coverage and the tax ceiling to impute nominal earnings. Our method differs from Fox's in that incomes for people who attained the earnings ceiling in the first quarter of the year were smoothed using adjacent years' earnings.

For ages 58 through 60 we combined the earnings obtained from the modified Fox method with earnings reported by the individual in the LRHS. To illustrate the procedure we followed, take the case of an individual who worked in 1968 and whose earnings reached the Social Security taxable maximum in the third quarter of the year. Had he reached the maximum at the beginning of the third quarter, his annual earnings would have been $15,599, whereas had he reached the maximum at the very end of the third quarter, his earnings would have been $10,374. If his reported earnings in the LRHS were between $10,374 and $15,599, the reported figure was used. But if reported earnings were outside the range $10,374 to $15,499, the appropriate boundary value was used. For 1970 a corresponding procedure was followed. For 1969, however, earnings information was not available in the LRHS. Thus we approximated 1969 LRHS earnings by the mean of 1968 LRHS earnings and 1970 LRHS earnings and followed an analogous procedure involving the modified Fox method. For subsequent years earnings were assumed to grow at the then-prevailing annual inflation rate of 4.8 percent. Earnings were then reduced by the relevant income tax and Social Security payroll tax.

Social Security Benefits of the Husband We regard the retirement decision as being made around age 60. The men in our sample turned age 60 around 1970. Congress at that time had already mandated increases in Social Security through 1972. Accordingly we assumed that our sample workers planned according to the 1972 Social Security rules in computing their initial Social Security benefits.

It would have been unreasonable for such persons to have assumed that Social Security benefits would remain at the 1972 levels. There had been increases in these benefits at frequent intervals, averaging about 3 percent per year in real terms over the 1960s. Those increases pertained both to first-year benefits and to the benefits received by individuals who were already Social Security beneficiaries. Consequently in constructing Social Security benefits, we assumed that our sample workers would have figured on future increases of similar magnitude.

Social Security benefits were calculated from formulas given in the *Social Security Bulletin Annual Statistical Supplement*. Three steps were involved: (1) calculating average monthly wage from data on Social Security earnings for all years since 1951, excluding the lowest five years of earnings; (2) computing Primary Insurance Amount using 1972 rules; and (3) computing benefit amount = Primary Insurance Amount times some multiple, where the multiple = 1.00 at age 65, is reduced by 5/9 percent for each month before age 65 that the individual retires, and is increased by 1/12 percent for each month after age 65 that the individual retires.

Social Security Benefits of the Wife The wife was assumed to begin receiving benefits at the same time as her husband, provided she was old enough to be eligible (62). If the wife was age 65 or older when her husband retired, she received 50 percent of his PIA at age 65. If she began collecting benefits between ages 62 and 65, she received 50 percent of her husband's PIA at age 65, less 25/36 percent times the number of months prior to age 65 that the benefits began.

Private Pension Benefits This is the weakest aspect of the LRHS. Kotlikoff and Smith (1983, table 4.5.31) present the annual pension benefits at age 65 for a $10,000 earner by industry as of 1977. The individuals in our sample would have been age 65 around that time. Kotlikoff and Smith's table is the best available approximation to pension benefit amounts, even though it requires us to assume that workers correctly foresaw future pension benefits in earlier years when they were deciding when to retire. We therefore assigned to each individual the pension benefit in the industry he was working in 1969 (assuming that his 1969 employer would be the source of any private pension benefit for which he might be eligible). For retirement at other ages, pension adjustment factors derived from Schulz and Leavitt were applied. We then reduced all pension amounts by the income tax to yield a net private pension benefit for each year. We entered this amount if the individual reported he was eligible for pension benefits in the year in question, and zero otherwise. Zero post-retirement private pension growth was assumed.

Present Discounted Values Present discounted values were obtained by discounting the appropriate annual figure by a 2 percent real discount rate and by the appropriate mortality factor, then summing.

The BAS

Constructing the elements of each worker's intertemporal budget set required detailed calculations, which were similar in parts to the computations performed on the LRHS. The main features of each component are the following.

Earnings Earnings imputations were based on reported earnings up to the Social Security tax ceiling as before, combined with the modification of the Fox routine. Real earnings after age 60 were predicted to age 68 using individual-specific equations to incorporate heterogeneity, which might be important since we have no measures of health in this data set. Earnings were then reduced by the relevant income and Social Security payroll taxes.

Social Security Benefits of the Husband In constructing Social Security benefits, we used the algorithms described for the LRHS. As earlier, we also assume that sample workers would have figured on future real benefit increases of the same magnitudes as for the LRHS.

Social Security Benefits of the Wife The BAS file did not contain consistent information on marital status because in some pension plans, the presence or absence of a wife is immaterial to the size of the pension benefit the worker receives. Without knowing if the worker was married, it was impossible to take account of wife's Social Security benefits.

Private Pension Benefits The strong suit of the BAS data set is its rich information on private pension benefit structures. The data available to us on pension plan formulas were provided to the Department of Labor in 1978. Not all of the descriptions were for that year exactly; however, all descriptions from that source described the pension rules in effect several years after 1970, the year in which our sample workers are supposed to have made their retirement decisions. It did not seem reasonable to assume that these workers had perfect foresight about what the pension rules were going to be in their companies as many as eight years later. Instead we went back to other sources to determine the rules that were in effect in 1970. These sources included the Labor Department's *Digest of Selected Pension Plans* for various years, union contracts, and, for some plans, historical information contained in the SPDs. The 1970 rules then served as a baseline for subsequent calculations.

Although the 1970 rules were useful, they were insufficient. In many plans pension benefits had been increased over the years. For example, in one of the pension plans, the monthly benefit at age 65 for a retiree with 30 years of service was $67.50 ($2.25/mo./yr. of service $\times$ 30 yrs. of service) in 1958. By 1972, it had increased to $230 ($7.50/mo./yr. of service $\times$ 30 yrs. of service). This 233 percent increase exceeded the rate of inflation, which was 45 percent over that fourteen year period. Put differently pension benefits had increased in that plan at a real rate of 3.4 percent per year. Since this had happened in the 1960s, we assumed that pensions would continue to increase in the 1970s and constructed the pension formulas accordingly. Specifically we increased the 1970 pension formula by the real rate of pension increase experienced in that pension plan during the 1960s. These increases were assumed to hold for as long as the worker was working. A different adjustment process occurred once the worker retired. In many pension plans, retirees receive the same nominal pension benefits for the remainder of their lives; however, some pension plans grant postretirement pension increases. In the auto industry, for instance, increases in pension benefits for retirees are written into union contracts. Hence we started from the assumption that postretirement increases were zero unless we had reason to believe otherwise. Five of the pension plans ended up with postretirement increases.

Initially we anticipated that it would be sufficient to develop a few benefit formulas into which most plans could be categorized; further exploration revealed otherwise. To illustrate, for many years the United Auto Workers have negotiated a defined benefit pension in which benefits appear to be a simple function of years of service. Nonetheless a close reading of pension contracts and SPDs indicates that the benefit structure is quite complex when due account is taken of the interaction of age and service. The benefit formula negotiated in the early 1970s, when the workers in our sample were about 60 years of age and presumably were deciding when to retire, provided pension amounts that varied depending on age and/or years of service. The following rules applied to an individual who had started work at company X at age 30.

1. Retiring after age 60 but before age 62: His pension benefit is $4,800 per year until age 62 and $5,400 per year from 62 to 64; thereafter it is [$90 × yrs. of service less (0.04 × the difference between the retirement age and 62)] + $63.60 (or $2,548 if the worker retires at age 60).

2. Retiring after age 62 but before age 65: His pension benefit is $5,400 per year until age 65; thereafter it is [$90 × yrs. of service] + $63.60 (or $2,944 if the worker retires at age 62).

3. Retiring at age 65 or later: His pension benefit is [$90 × yrs. of service] + $63.60 (or $3,214 if the worker retires at age 65).

Benefits in 1 and 3 are available only after completing ten years of service. One remarkable feature of this private pension structure is that at age 65, a retiree actually gets less in initial pension benefits per year than at earlier ages. An explanation for this is that the pension plan is de facto integrated with Social Security; although benefits are not formally reduced when Social Security recipiency begins, the perception is that workers can claim full Social Security benefits at age 65 and thus are provided with supplemental private benefits until Social Security commences. Clearly the benefit formula cannot be summarized by a simple function of age and service.

Pension descriptions for the other plans were devised in a similar manner and transformed into computer algorithms; more detail on the individual plans is given in chapter 4. The final sample of plans cannot be identified for confidentiality reasons; however, we can reveal that the group includes four blue-collar plans negotiated with the United Auto Workers, several non-union manufacturing plans, and a few service sector plans. All were defined benefit pensions in effect during the 1970s.

Present Discounted Values Present discounted values were obtained by discounting the appropriate annual figures by a 2 percent real discount rate and by the appropriate mortality factor, then summing.

3. The Shape of the Intertemporal Budget Set

The intertemporal budget set is the present discounted value of future lifetime income (PDVY) that a worker would expect to receive for alternate retirement ages. In this section, we present the intertemporal budget set for a worker turning 60 around 1970. We calculate the PDVY profile as well as the profiles of the components: earnings (PDVE), private pension (PDVPP), and Social Security (PDVSS). Some previous researchers have examined the PDVPP and

PDVSS paths; our results for those variables should be viewed as providing additional evidence in controversial areas. However, no one else has combined earnings, private pensions, and Social Security into a unified PDVY measure despite its clear importance from a theoretical perspective. Our evidence on the PDVY profile is therefore novel in the retirement literature.

We begin with the results for the LRHS and then turn to the BAS.

The LRHS Sample

Table 3.1 presents the elements of the lifetime budget set. These figures were calculated for each worker in the LRHS sample and then averaged. They are expressed in constant 1970 dollars.

We begin with an examination of the age 60 column. The budget set is calculated looking forward from age 60. An individual who retires at age 60 would earn nothing from that age onward. Hence PDVE is zero at that age. However, he and his wife would have received Social Security benefits beginning at age 62. (All men in our LRHS sample were married.) After discounting for time preference and for mortality risk, the present discounted value of expected Social Security benefits would have amounted to $31,727. This is the PDVSS entry in the age 60 column. Some LRHS retirees would have received a private pension if they retired at age 60. These pension amounts, weighted by the probability of receiving them, would have yielded a present discounted value of $3,075. Taken together, the present discounted value of his total income (PDVY) from earnings, Social Security, and private pensions
would have been $34,802 for retirement at age 60.

ment at age 60 with retirement at age 65. If we look
in the table and compare these values with the age-60
present discounted value of net real earnings would
ment was postponed. This is obvious, reflecting the
nted value of earnings cumulates the preceding annual
ing them.
ted value of net real Social Security benefits for the
uld have increased by about $15,000 if retirement were
to 65. This is because the extra earnings during the
ted into higher annual benefits that more than made up
enefits from working one year longer. This feature held
0s, when the LRHS workers were making their retire-
as since been undone by the 1977 amendments to the
hich stopped increasing real Social Security benefits.
caveats about the quality of the LRHS data, here is what

Table 3.1
Elements of the retirement budget set around 1970 for LRHS sample: Average present values of earnings, Social Security, and private pensions at alternative retirement ages (N = 1024) (1970 $)

Present Discounted values	Retirement Age								
	60	61	62	63	64	65	66	67	68
(1) Earnings [PDVE]	$0	$7,048	$13,741	$20,085	$26,098	$31,727	$36,941	$41,823	$46,382
(2) Social Security [PDVSS][a]	31,727	33,029	34,514	38,417	42,389	46,230	48,046	49,610	50,904
(3) Private pension [PDVPP]	3,075	3,282	4,243	5,520	5,232	5,226	5,445	5,068	4,619
(4) Income [PDVY = (1) + (2) + (3)]	34,802 ~	43,359 ~	52,498 ~	64,023 ~	73,719 ~	83,184 ~	90,432 ~	96,501 ~	101,905
Change in PDVY		8,557	9,139	11,525	9,696	9,465	7,248	6,069	5,404

a. Social Security benefits are computed assuming the individual retires in the year in question and files for benefits when first eligible.

Table 3.2
Imputed private pension amounts, LRHS sample

	Retirement Age								
	60	61	62	63	64	65	66	67	68
Private pension benefit if eligible ($)	1,969	2,050	2,136	2,225	2,318	2,415	2,517	2,624	2,737
Eligibility rate	.169	.194	.272	.389	.398	.432	.490	.498	.498

they show. The present discounted value of net real private pension benefits would have been some $2,000 higher had the average worker retired at age 65 rather than age 60. Table 3.2 displays the average pension benefits per year if the worker is eligible, as well as the proportions eligible for pensions at each age. Eligibility rates increase sharply, and this interacts with higher benefits per year, more than offsetting the loss of pension benefits up to age 63. But after age 63 most of the workers who would ever be eligible for pensions were eligible already. Also, annual benefit amounts do not increase as fast after age 63. The result is that the net present discounted value of private pension benefits would have declined from age 63 onward for the average LRHS worker.

The present discounted value of net real total income would have been nearly $50,000 higher for the average LRHS worker had he retired at age 65 rather than at age 60. Of this $50,000, the bulk of it (around 65 percent) would have been due to higher PDV of earnings, most of the rest (about 30 percent) to higher PDV of Social Security benefits, and only a small part (about 5 percent) to higher PDV of private pension benefits.

Finally, since we will be concentrating on PDVY, let us focus on row 4 in table 3.1. Two additional points stand out in the LRHS data. First, PDVY would always have increased as retirement was postponed. Total income over expected remaining lifetime would have been three times higher for retirement at age 68 than at age 60. It always would have paid the worker in monetary terms to go on working. Second, PDVY would have increased unevenly. These differences are shown beneath row 4. Deferring retirement from age 62 to age 63 would have added more than $11,000 to PDVY—more than double the monetary gain to working from age 67 to age 68, which is just $5,400.

These observations on PDVY—that it increased as retirement was post-

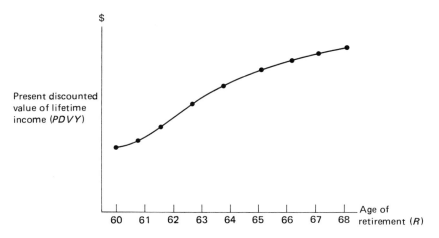

Figure 3.1
Present discounted value of total income (PDVY) as viewed from age 60 for alternate
retirement ages, the LRHS worker

poned but the increases were uneven—produce a budget set such as shown in
figure 3.1. That the resultant pattern is monotonic but not smooth has important implications for estimating the effects of the budget set on retirement
ages. We return to this point in chapter 6.

Plan-by-Plan Data in the BAS

The intertemporal budget set for the BAS sample is based on information
drawn from ten pension plans. The plan-by-plan data represent a bewildering
amount of information. We content ourselves at this juncture with a few
observations on each plan and then move to aggregated tables. Further
analysis of individual pension plans appears in chapter 4.

Tables 3.3 through 3.6 present plan-by-plan data on the PDVs of earnings,
Social Security, private pensions, and total income for the average worker in
each of the ten plans. Four conclusions emerge from these tables.

1. Average earnings streams are quite similar across the ten plans, except for
plan 5, in which earnings are markedly lower. This suggests that older
workers in these plans do not receive very different wage payoffs if they defer
retirement.

2. Average Social Security benefit flows are even more similar. This is to be
expected because earnings are the major determinant of Social Security benefits, earnings differences across plans are not large, and such earnings dif-

Table 3.3
Plan-level BAS data: Present value of net earnings for alternative retirement ages

	Retirement Age								
	60	61	62	63	64	65	66	67	68
Plan 1	$0	$7,022	$13,950	$20,625	$26,920	$32,905	$38,571	$43,900	$48,904
Plan 2	0	7,036	13,983	20,883	27,616	34,094	40,261		
Plan 3	0	7,522	14,856	21,856	28,466	34,714			
Plan 4	0	7,477	14,943	22,229	29,169	35,753	42,022	47,922	53,507
Plan 5	0	5,403	10,672	15,839	20,721	25,231	29,476	33,426	37,100
Plan 6	0	7,496	14,633	21,520	28,153	34,434			
Plan 7	0	8,477	16,821	24,972	33,045	40,732			
Plan 8	0	9,378	18,569	27,400	35,850	43,883	51,466	58,611	65,330
Plan 9	0	6,694	13,653	20,752	28,404	35,491	42,291	48,730	54,811
Plan 10	0	8,213	16,168	23,993	31,465	38,562			

Note: Empty cells cannot be computed due to mandatory retirement provisions

Table 3.4
Plan-level BAS data: Present value of Social Security for alternative retirement ages

	Retirement Age								
	60	61	62	63	64	65	66	67	68
Plan 1	$28,589	$29,529	$30,412	$31,930	$33,304	$34,332	$33,203	$31,947	$30,651
Plan 2	28,688	29,750	30,731	32,348	33,810	34,928	33,831		
Plan 3	28,786	29,761	30,697	32,230	33,618	34,670			
Plan 4	28,895	29,844	30,750	32,289	33,681	34,728	33,584	32,300	30,863
Plan 5	27,187	28,081	28,869	30,229	31,456	32,378	31,252	29,998	28,626
Plan 6	28,530	29,555	30,479	32,010	33,393	34,432			
Plan 7	26,635	27,743	28,821	30,523	32,078	33,338			
Plan 8	29,264	30,159	31,057	32,616	34,035	35,087	33,948	32,643	31,193
Plan 9	28,432	29,411	30,294	31,842	33,245	34,357	33,255	32,005	30,610
Plan 10	28,616	29,558	30,443	31,958	33,337	34,395			

Note: Empty cells cannot be computed due to mandatory retirement provisions.

Table 3.5
Plan-level BAS data: Present value of net pension benefits for alternative retirement ages

	60	61	62	63	64	65	66	67	68
Plan 1	$28,879	$28,425	$28,008	$26,290	$24,699	$23,355	$22,811	$22,181	$21,503
Plan 2	35,200	35,313	35,584	35,457	35,067	34,558	33,900		
Plan 3	33,595	32,740	32,232	30,227	28,452	26,904			
Plan 4	30,390	29,720	29,359	27,653	26,035	24,651	24,073	23,383	22,603
Plan 5	0	0	1,058	2,018	3,132	7,123	7,159	6,740	6,228
Plan 6	10,939	11,739	17,518	16,658	15,705	14,682			
Plan 7	22,383	22,623	22,537	22,286	21,921	21,297			
Plan 8	30,621	32,201	32,929	31,969	30,980	30,193	28,776	27,146	25,383
Plan 9	17,655	17,488	17,292	17,037	16,690	16,902	16,190	15,812	15,358
Plan 10	19,256	17,341	15,480	14,970	14,492	13,876			

Note: Empty cells cannot be computed due to mandatory retirement provisions.

Table 3.6
Plan-level BAS data: Present value of total income for alternative retirement ages

	Retirement Age								
	60	61	62	63	64	65	66	67	68
Plan 1	$57,468	$64,977	$72,370	$78,845	$84,923	$90,592	$94,586	$98,028	$100,968
Plan 2	63,888	72,099	80,298	88,689	96,493	103,580	107,992		
Plan 3	62,381	70,023	77,785	84,313	90,535	96,288			
Plan 4	59,285	67,041	75,051	82,171	88,885	95,132	99,679	103,605	106,974
Plan 5	27,187	33,484	40,599	48,086	55,308	64,733	67,887	70,165	71,955
Plan 6	39,469	48,789	62,629	70,189	77,251	83,547			
Plan 7	49,018	58,842	68,179	77,781	87,043	95,366			
Plan 8	59,885	71,738	82,555	91,985	100,864	109,163	114,189	118,401	121,906
Plan 9	46,088	53,593	61,239	69,631	78,340	86,750	91,735	96,546	100,779
Plan 10	47,872	55,112	62,091	70,921	79,294	86,833			

Note: Empty cells cannot be computed due to mandatory retirement provisions.

ferences as there are are narrowed even further by deliberate equalization of benefits in the Social Security benefit computation formula.

3. Private pension benefits vary across plans quite a bit. Differences appear both in levels and in tilts (the rate at which they reward continued work). Regarding levels, pension benefits are many times higher in plan 2, for example, than in plan 5. The tilts also differ. Plans 5 and 6 are among those that offer substantial gains in pension values for continued work. Many other plans do the opposite.

4. In every plan, PDVY increases substantially as retirement is postponed. Our general conclusion from the plan-by-plan evidence is that PDVYs vary across pension plans primarily because of differences in the level and tilt of pension benefits rather than because of differences in other components of the intertemporal budget set.

The BAS and the LRHS: A Comparison

Let us examine the intertemporal budget set for all BAS workers taken together and compare it with the LRHS. The relevant data appear in table 3.7. We find the following similarities and differences:

1. In the BAS sample, the present discounted value of net real earnings would have increased as retirement was postponed, just as in the LRHS and for the same reason.

2. Earnings in the two samples are similar. The BAS workers earn only about 5 to 10 percent more.

3. The present discounted value of Social Security benefits is greater for the LRHS sample than for the BAS sample. This is because the LRHS sample includes wives' benefits (all LRHS workers were married) and the BAS sample does not (because marital status was unknown for large numbers of workers, so the figures include workers' benefits only).[4]

4. In the BAS, the present discounted value of net real Social Security benefits would have increased by about $6,000 (or 21 percent) if retirement was postponed from age 60 to age 65. This increase is due to higher worker benefits derived from deferring retirement. This contrasts with LRHS, where the gain was larger because increased wives' benefits were also included.

5. Private pensions in the BAS are several times higher on average than in the LRHS. Pension coverage is partly responsible: all of the BAS workers would receive pension benefits, compared with 17 percent of the LRHS workers if they retired at age 60 and 43 percent if they retired at age 65. But these percentages do not explain the whole difference. If the LRHS pension data are to be believed, we might infer that the pension plans contained in our

Table 3.7
Elements of retirement budget set around 1970 for BAS sample: Average present values of earnings, Social Security, and private pensions at alternative retirement ages in ten plans (N = 8,733) (1970 $)

Present Discounted Values	Retirement Age					
	60	61	62	63	64	65
(1) Earnings [PDVE]	$0	$7,472	$14,825	$22,007	$28,981	$35,581
(2) Social Security [PDVSS][a]	28,363	29,339	30,256	31,798	33,196	34,265
(3) Private pension [PDVPP]	22,892	22,759	23,200	22,457	21,717	21,354
(4) Income [PDVY = (1) + (2) + (3)]	51,255	59,570	68,281	76,262	83,894	91,200
Change in PDVY:	8,345	8,711	7,981	7,632	7,306	

Note: Benefits are computed only until age 65 because some of the sample plans had mandatory retirement at that age.
a. Social Security benefits are computed assuming the individual retires in the year in question and files for benefits when first eligible.

BAS sample provide more generous pension benefits on average than do other pension plans. Given the crudeness of the pension figures in the LRHS, however, we prefer to remain agnostic on this issue.

6. The present discounted value of the net real private pension benefits (PDVPP) would have risen somewhat on average had the average worker in the BAS sample retired at age 62 instead of age 60 and diminished somewhat had he waited until 65 to retire. On average the PDVPP hill is very flat. But this average conceals a variety of plans with diverse patterns. Some reward continued work and some do not. This diversity is evident in table 3.7, where the flat hill in the BAS is seen. This contrasts with the LRHS, in which PDVPP continued to rise between ages 60 and 65, primarily because of rising eligibility rates.

7. The present value of net real total income would have been nearly $40,000 (about 80 percent) higher for the average worker in the BAS had he retired at age 65 rather than age 60. Ninety percent of this increase is attributable to increases in cumulative earnings and 15 percent to Social Security; private pension benefits contribute negatively because they fall in present value as the worker delays retirement. The gain in PDVY is smaller in both dollar terms and percentage terms than it was in the LRHS (approximately $50,000, or 150 percent). The tilt is less in the BAS than in the LRHS because Social Security benefits increase faster in present value terms in the LRHS than in the BAS.

Finally, since we concentrate on PDVY in our retirement analysis, we again highlight PDVY changes.

8. PDVY would always increase as retirement was postponed in the BAS sample. This replicates the pattern discerned in the LRHS data.

9. PDVY would have increased unevenly. These differences are shown beneath row 4 of table 3.7: deferring retirement from age 60 to age 61 would have generated over $8,300 more in PDVY, whereas the gain was only about $7,300 between ages 64 and 65. Nonlinearity in the BAS sample is illustrated in figure 3.2.

Readers are reminded that this study is the first to compute total discounted income streams from earnings, private pensions, and Social Security anticipated at each possible retirement age. For this reason our figures are not directly comparable with those reported in other studies of retiree incomes.

4. Summary

Our examination of the intertemporal income opportunities available to older workers was guided by two questions: (1) What would a typical worker

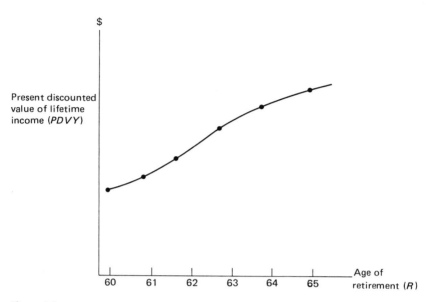

Figure 3.2
Present discounted value of total income (PDVY) as viewed from age 60 for alternate retirement ages, BAS worker

retiring at age 60 anticipate receiving in earnings, private pension, and Social Security benefits? (2) How would these income streams change if he were to defer retirement?

Two data sets were used to address these questions: the LRHS and the Labor Department's BAS. For the average worker, retirement at age 60 would have generated an income stream of about $35,000 in the LRHS data and about $51,000 in the BAS (in 1970 dollars). These amounts differ mainly because of the more important role played by private pensions in the BAS sample.

An examination of changes in income as retirement is postponed also suggests some interesting findings. First, private pensions vary widely in the way they reward deferred retirement. In some plans the expected present value of net pension benefits would have been expected to increase in real terms if a worker deferred retirement. In other plans benefits would fall if the worker waited to retire. Second, for both data sets examined, the present value of Social Security benefits would have been expected to increase if retirement were postponed. Third, the average older worker in both data files would always have added to his income by deferring retirement since the gain to postponing retirement was always positive in present value terms. Fourth, in general, the expected gains to deferring retirement, though always positive, were not uniform: working paid twice as much at some ages as at others.

4   Variation across Pension Plans

Pension plans differ substantially from one another. Some create powerful incentives toward earlier retirement; others do not. In this chapter we explore these differences in more detail.[1]

1. Methodology and Data

For the analysis in this chapter we employ only the BAS sample since the LRHS is weak on private pension variables. For the most part the calculations here parallel those already described; however, two differences are important: this chapter uses fourteen pension plans rather than ten and the calculations reported here are for a hypothetical illustrative worker rather than the cross-worker averages within each pension plan.

The explanation for these differences is as follows. Pension formulas could be derived in the BAS file for fourteen pension plans. Ten of these plans offered data on large numbers of retirees, ranging from 142 to 2,923 pension recipients. The remaining four plans had too few pension recipients in the BAS file because the match-up between pension rules and pension recipients was far from perfect. The missing data on retirees did not, however, preclude analysis of the pension plans themselves, so our analysis of differences in pension structure was based on the larger sample of fourteen plans. This procedure used an illustrative worker and calculated that worker's pension opportunities in each plan.

For purposes of comparison, it is useful to derive benefits using the same basic earnings and tenure characteristics so as to hold constant other factors that might vary across plans. It is important that this illustrative individual be similar to workers actually covered by the pension plan since benefit structures generally are constructed with a relevant salary range in mind. Others who have computed plan-specific pension benefits (Lazear, 1982; Kotlikoff and Smith, 1983) did not have such information and thus were required to assume a range of salary options to cover most of the possibilities.

The illustrative worker we develop was assigned the mean characteristics of the 8,733 BAS retirees described in chapter 3. Earnings are an important input to private pension benefit determination. The average earnings are those that appear in table 3.7. In addition, years of service are also taken into account in most plans, either in the benefit formula directly or in determining which of several different benefit formulas is applied. Therefore an assumption about years of service for the illustrative individual is also required. Average tenure was twenty-six years in our sample of pension beneficiaries; we used this tenure figure for the computations that follow. Interestingly this relatively long length of time on one's last job is compatible with Hall's (1982) recent discussion of lifetime jobs among males in the U.S. labor force, in which he found that half the men would have attained twenty or more years of service with their employers by the time they reached age 65. One characteristic that was not needed to calculate pension benefits was marital status, since none of the pension plans in our sample paid different pension benefits to married workers compared to single ones.[2]

Annual benefits were computed for the illustrative worker at each possible retirement age, in every pension plan. We determined the present value of all benefit streams by taking a forward-looking perspective: from the viewpoint of age 60, what is the discounted value of pension benefits available had the worker retired at 60, or 61, or later, until the mandatory retirement age?[3] We followed standard practice by discounting each year's benefits by the probability of mortality at each age, based on survival rate information for the cohort in question. In addition, we deflated future benefits by inflation and by a real discount rate. Estimated future benefit streams assumed continuation of the rate of price increases prevailing in the early 1970s; to discount benefits accruing in the future, we used the same nominal rate. In addition, a 2 percent real discount rate was used to reflect time preference. Confirmatory analysis was conducted with other discount rates and produced results virtually identical to those reported here.

The pension plans we analyzed are divided into two subsets for ease of discussion. Pattern plans are those in which benefits at any given retirement age are based exclusively on years of service with the firm. In conventional plans, benefits are determined not only by years of service with the firm but also by final salary. Pattern plans are most prevalent in situations where most of the workers in the pension plan receive equal pay for standardized work, as in large manufacturing establishments; conventional plans are more common when the pay is less standardized, as when workers or firms have discretion over work hours.

2. Results

Overall Patterns

Table 4.1 presents data for the illustrative worker for all fourteen pension plans averaged together.[4] The top panel presents average first-year private pension benefits available to a worker at each alternative retirement age between 60 and 65. In addition it indicates their magnitude relative to both Social Security and net, aftertax earnings, calculated according to the description in chapter 3.

One finding is that private pensions amount to 25 to 30 percent of preretirement after-tax earnings. The overall replacement rate, including both pensions and Social Security, is between 50 and 60 percent.

Another finding concerns the change in annual pension benefit levels as retirement is deferred from age 60 to 65. The worker retiring at age 60 would, on average, receive a pension benefit during that year of about $2,200; if he deferred retirement by one year, the addition to (nominal) first-year benefits would be on the order of 7 percent. The marginal payoff to an additional year is by no means uniform across retirement ages, however. Benefits available at age 62 are lower on average than for age 61. This rather peculiar benefit decline can be explained by noting that some pension plans provide supplemental income until the age of eligibility for Social Security. (Reduced benefits are first available at age 62, full benefits at age 65.) Indeed the lowering of annual benefits between ages 61 and 62 is repeated again between ages 64 and 65. Therefore the annual marginal payoff to retiring one year later varies quite a lot across retirement ages, a fact not immediately obvious from a superficial review of the benefit regulations.

Table 4.1 also indicates that the patterns discerned for the annual benefit amounts are quite different from the present value pattern. Although first-year benefits payable to an age 60 retiree are much lower than to an age 61 retiree, the age 60 retiree nonetheless receives a somewhat higher lifetime benefit stream. On the other hand, from age 62 on, although first-year pension benefits increase as retirement is postponed, the present value of benefits decreases because the reduced pay-out period overcomes the higher annual benefit. To summarize, the change in present value of benefits between 60 and 61 is −1 percent; between 61 and 62, +5 percent; between 62 and 63, −2 percent; between 63 and 64, −2 percent; and between 64 and 65, −2 percent.

The reward structure inherent in private pension plans varies for different retirement ages. Overall it encourages postponing retirement from age 61 to age 62; thereafter benefits appear to decline slowly as the individual works

Table 4.1
Private pensions, Social Security benefits, and earnings at alternative retirement ages for an illustrative individual in fourteen pension plans, BAS data

	Retirement Age					
	60	61	62	63	64	65
Annual amounts (nominal $)						
Net pension (first year)	$2,190	$2,350	$2,322	$2,513	$2,724	$2,634
Social Security (first year)	1,858	1,916	1,973	2,333	2,749	3,209
Net earnings	7,947	8,254	8,717	9,185	9,563	9,760
Present value amounts (1970 $)						
Net pension (PDVPP)	$19,071	18,960	19,953	19,493	19,029	18,542

Source: Based on pension algorithms for fourteen plans and computed for illustrative worker.

each additional year. On average benefits appear to be just short of actuarially neutral after age 62. The changes involved are quite small; the pension hill is very flat.

Variability across Pension Plans

Present values in table 4.1 are averages of several different underlying structures. It is of interest to look behind the averages. Table 4.2 provides more detail. In the first row the overall figures are repeated; the next rows separate the plans into two groups: pattern plans and conventional plans.

It is evident that the overall means in fact obscure some key differences between the two kinds of benefit structures. Pattern plans tend to structure their first-year benefits so that they rise more or less smoothly until age 64; annual benefits typically fall for workers deferring benefits beyond that point. Conventional plans' first-year benefits work quite differently, since here benefits for the age 62 retiree are lower than for the worker leaving one year earlier. After age 62, however, conventional plans tend to provide ever-increasing benefit amounts for workers postponing retirement, up to age 65.

Breaking out present values of benefits for these two types of plans suggests an even stronger contrast. Pattern plans discourage work beyond age 60. An employee in a pattern plan who defers retiring until age 65 will receive lifetime benefits about 18 percent lower than at age 60. On the other hand, conventional plans' present value streams are structured so that the worker who defers retirement until age 65 will receive about 17 percent higher benefits than if he retired at 60. Thus between ages 60 and 65, conventional pension plans appear to improve benefits by about the same amount as pattern plans reduce them.

Clearly the overall incentives differ between the two types of plans. To see whether marginal incentives are smooth or erratic, we compute changes in pension present values for each additional year of work:

Change in Retirement Age

Change in PDVPP	61–61	61–62	62–63	63–64	64–65
Pattern	-2%	-2%	-5%	-5%	-5%
Conventional	$+2$	$+14$	$+0$	$+0$	$+0$

Evidently pattern plans actively encourage early retirement, whereas conventional plans encourage prolonged work until age 62. After age 62 conventional plans provide a rather flat payoff schedule for additional years'

Table 4.2
Net private pension amounts at alternative retirement ages for an illustrative worker in pattern plans and conventional plans, BAS data

	Retirement Age					
	60	61	62	63	64	65
Annual net pension benefits (nominal $)						
Overall mean	$2,190	$2,350	$2,322	$2,513	$2,742	$2,634
Pattern plan mean	2,653	2,760	2,907	3,059	3,214	2,626
Conventional plan mean	1,728	1,939	1,883	2,103	2,356	2,639
PDVPP (1970 $)						
Overall mean	19,070	18,960	19,953	19,493	19,029	18,542
Pattern plan mean	24,795	24,192	23,787	22,617	21,432	20,275
Conventional plan mean	14,777	15,036	17,078	17,150	17,227	17,243

Source: Based on pension algorithms for fourteen plans as applied to the illustrative worker.

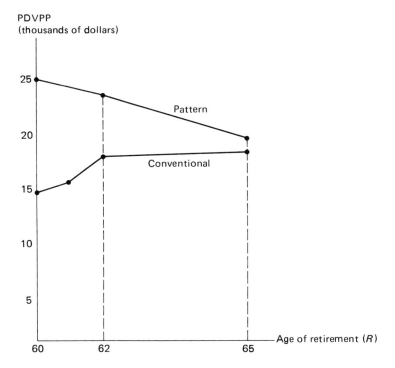

Figure 4.1
Present value of private pension benefits: Pattern plans and conventional plans

work, whereas in pattern plans, the slope becomes strongly negative (see figure 4.1).

This diversity in the way pensions reward work at older ages contrasts with a view widely held based on the work of Burkhauser and Turner (1982) and Lazear (1982). In Lazear's words, "Most workers receive pensions, the expected present value of which declines as retirement is postponed . . . . This evidence suggests that firms attempt to buy old workers out of their long-term arrangement" (p. 20–21). Our data show that some pensions do exhibit this feature, providing the highest present values for early retirement, but others do not.[5]

Detailed Pension Plan Analysis

Table 4.3 provides a breakdown of the individual pension plans' benefit structures so as to reveal in greater detail the variability in economic rewards for continued work. These plan-specific data permit the computation of

Table 4.3
Plan-level BAS data: Present values of net private pension benefits for alternative retirement ages

	Retirement Age								
	60	61	62	63	64	65	66	67	68
Pattern plans									
UAW plans									
Plan 1	*$28,181*	$27,586	$27,189	$25,455	$23,787	$22,195	$21,706	$21,140	$20,500
Plan 2	36,030	36,146	36,599	36,341	35,730	34,987	34,081		
Plan 3	28,176	27,571	27,189	25,455	23,787	22,195	21,706	21,140	20,500
Plan 4	28,176	27,571	27,189	25,455	23,787	22,195	21,706	21,140	20,500
Non-UAW plans									
Plan 11	*21,858*	19,814	17,912	16,147	14,512	13,001	11,608	10,328	9,153
Plan 12	6,351	6,464	6,641	6,850	6,986	7,079	6,620	6,156	5,692
Conventional plans									
Plan 5	0	0	9,300	10,027	10,087	*10,497*	9,461	8,891	7,951
Plan 6	13,527	14,176	20,471	19,364	18,173	16,869			
Plan 7	16,410	16,709	16,841	16,977	*17,028*	16,893			
Plan 8	20,012	20,256	20,270	19,335	18,359	17,246	16,190	15,081	13,841
Plan 9	14,851	15,079	15,290	15,504	16,318	*17,174*	16,563	15,866	15,109
Plan 13	17,671	19,669	21,594	23,468	25,295	26,981			
Plan 14	16,256	17,042	17,668	18,291	18,810	*19,084*			
Plan 10	19,491	17,354	15,193	14,230	13,742	13,198	12,605	11,592	10,950

Notes: Italicized figures are row maxima. Empty cells indicate retirement is mandatory in that plan at that age. Plans numbers 1 through 10 used in empirical analysis of chapters 4 through 6 and 9.
Source: Based on pension algorithms as applied to illustrative worker.

benefit streams for ages beyond 65 in cases where continued work was permitted; firms with mandatory retirement are indicated by empty cells.

This disaggregate analysis suggest several conclusions. One is that the pattern plans as a whole, and UAW plans in particular, definitely encourage early retirement; except for plan 12, the present values of net pension amounts in pattern plans attain their maxima between ages 60 and 62. Therefore the individual plan-level data confirm the earlier observation that pattern plans offer incentives favoring earlier retirement. Evidence for conventional plans is more mixed. In one plan, the present value of pension benefits peaks at age 60, two peak at age 62, one at 64, and the remainder at age 65. Thus most of the conventional plans tend to encourage later retirement.

3. Summary

In-depth analysis of pension plans and their beneficiaries has generated several interesting conclusions. First, the marginal payoffs to deferring retirement are quite uneven. Some pension plans are structured so that an additional year of work at older ages adds to lifetime benefits; others do just the opposite. Second, the two types of defined benefit pension plans examined differ in their overall incentive patterns. Pattern plans (those based just on years of service) appear to encourage early retirement; conventional plans (those that use final salary as well as years of service) tend to reward later retirement. Finally, plan-level data indicate a great deal of cross-plan variability in the way benefits are structured.

III Retirement Responses to Income Opportunities

Previous chapters framed a theoretical approach to the retirement decision and described in detail the elements of older workers' budget sets. In this part we estimate the empirical effect of economic variables on the age of retirement.

The next four chapters apply several different econometric models to the BAS and LRHS data. Since we have few a priori notions about precise functional forms, we adopt an eclectic approach, which compares several different models to ascertain the sensitivity of findings to model specification.

Chapter 5 presents and evaluates a linear regression model of the retirement decision. In Chapter 6 two discrete choice models are estimated using a logit framework. The regression model and both logit models require specific assumptions about the underlying distribution of tastes; in this sense they are both parametric approaches. In contrast, chapter 7 develops a nonparametric method for evaluating the economic determinants of retirement patterns. The predictions of the models are compared in chapter 8.

In all models, our theoretical approach finds empirical support: economic opportunities affect retirement ages. A second finding also emerges strongly from both data sets: the estimated elasticities are not large.

5   Regression Models

The theoretical framework of part I and the budget sets developed in part II can be combined in various ways to evaluate how economic variables affect retirement ages. This chapter reports the results of estimating a retirement equation using linear regression analysis. The model builds on our earlier theoretical analysis by focusing on the decision variable over which older workers have most control: the age of retirement. In addition it improves on previous empirical studies by incorporating the complex institutional features of older workers' income opportunities.

The regression approach permits the development and testing of two empirical propositions about how the intertemporal budget set affects retirement behavior: wealthier people are expected to retire earlier, and people who anticipate greater financial rewards from deferring retirement should retire later. Our findings confirm these propositions in both the BAS and LRHS data sets.

1. Model Specification

The theoretical model developed in chapter 2 generated several predictions about how retirement ages would respond to changes in earnings, pension, or Social Security income. In this chapter we parameterize the budget set by a linear function, the intercept of which is the present discounted value of expected Social Security and private pension income if the worker retired at age 60 (PDVY60) and the slope of which is the change in present discounted value of those benefits and earnings if the worker defers retirement from age 60 to age 65 (YSLOPE65). This parameterization leads to two hypotheses.

Hypothesis 1 The age of retirement will be a negative function of PDVY60. This prediction relies on three arguments. First, if leisure is a normal good, an ordinary wealth effect would cause wealthier people to consume more leisure years, thus retiring earlier. Second, wealthier people probably value extra income less than poorer people do because of diminishing marginal utility of income. Third, in a household production context, wealthier people are likely to own more goods complementary with leisure and hence may have higher marginal utility of leisure years than do less well-off persons. Empirically, then, we expect wealthier people to retire earlier.

YSLOPE65 affects retirement in theoretically ambiguous ways because of offsetting income and substitution effects, as in static hours of work models. On the one hand, higher anticipated earnings, private pension, and Social Security payments in the future make the individual richer for all ages after the base year. This should induce more consumption of leisure and hence earlier retirement, by an ordinary income effect. On the other hand, when expected future earnings and retirement benefit slopes are higher, the early retiree forgoes more income. This creates a substitution effect in the direction of more years of work, hence later retirement. Although it is an empirical question as to which effect is stronger, we expect there to be an inverse relation between the demand for leisure and its price. Hence we have:

Hypothesis 2 Although theory is ambiguous, we expect to find empirically that people who have more to gain by deferring retirement do postpone retirement. Therefore the age of retirement is expected to be a positive function of YSLOPE.

We test these propositions directly by regressing retirement ages chosen by older workers, against their values of PDVY60 and YSLOPE65. Hence, the model evaluated in this chapter takes the general form, $RETAGE_i = c_0 + c_1 PDVY60_i + c_2 YSLOPE65_i + e_i$, where e_i is a disturbance term assumed to be normally distributed across individuals. In order for the ordinary least-squares model to apply, any omitted variables must be uncorrelated with the individual-specific error term; furthermore, the e_i's must be independent of income variables on the right-hand side of the equation. In the present context this requires that workers' unobserved tastes for retirement income be uncorrelated with income levels or income gains if retirement were postponed. Whether these assumptions hold cannot be tested directly in this model. Other chapters develop alternative approaches to test whether results are robust.

2. Empirical Results

Table 5.1 contains findings for the BAS sample on the question of how earnings, private pensions, and Social Security benefits affect the retirement age decision. Column 1 shows that the predictions suggested by theory are confirmed in the BAS data set. The coefficient on *PDVY60* is negative and significantly different from zero, indicating that persons with more base year

Table 5.1
Retirement age regressions for pooled BAS sample ($N = 8733$)

| | Dependent Variable: Age of Retirement | | |
	(1)	(2)	(3)
Variable			
Constant	64.17*	64.52*	65.40*
	(748.94)	(626.56)	(125.71)
PDVY60 (in thousands of dollars)	−.039*	−.034*	−.103*
	(32.71)	(24.15)	(5.30)
YSLOPE65 (in thousands of dollars)	.030*	.029*	.055*
	(23.60)	(22.92)	(6.84)
Intercept dummies		a	a
Slope dummies			a
R^2	.16	.27	.33

Note: t statistics are shown in parentheses.
* Statistically significant at the .05 level.
a Statistically significant by conventional F tests.

income retire earlier. In addition, the effect of YSLOPE65 is positive, indicating that individuals who have more to gain by deferring retirement do in fact retire later.[1]

For the workers in the BAS sample, 16 percent of the variance in retirement ages is accounted for by just these two economic variables, a high R^2 for microdata. The last two columns of table 5.1 indicate that even more explanatory power is provided when plan-specific dummy variables are entered (column 2) and then also when plan-specific slope-shift terms are included (column 3).

Similar qualitative conclusions flow from the empirical regression results obtained with LRHS data. Using the PDVY60 and YSLOPE65 variables already defined, we find the following (t statistics in parentheses):

$$RETAGE = 64.68 - .0308 \ PDVY60 + .0058 \ YSLOPE65, \quad R^2 = 0.02. \tag{6.1}$$
$$\quad (4.6) \qquad \qquad (1.6)$$

As before, PDVY60 exhibits a significantly negative coefficient, confirming that retirement years are a normal good. In fact, the magnitude of the response is virtually identical to the corresponding regression on the BAS sample. YSLOPE65 has the expected positive sign and is significantly greater than zero at conventional significance levels. The positive sign of the variable confirms that people who have more to gain by retiring later do in fact defer retirement.

The proportion of variance explained is quite a bit lower in the LRHS data set than in the BAS for the corresponding regression. We attribute this to the better quality of the pension data in the BAS compared to the LRHS. For this reason the empirical work often emphasizes the findings derived from the BAS sample containing detailed information on pension plan variables. Nonetheless, it is also useful to determine the extent to which the LRHS sample replicates the BAS findings since the LRHS has the advantage of being a representative sample of older males. To the extent that both samples tell a similar story about older workers' retirement decision making, our results are strengthened.

The significance of the plan-level dummy variables in the BAS sample (table 5.1) suggests the possibility that workers in different pension plans may be differentially responsive to the economic incentives associated with deferred retirement. Unfortunately very few variables were available with which this hypothesis could be explored further using the BAS data set. In some plans race and marital status were listed but proved to have no significant impact on our findings. With regard to firm-side factors, we were able to develop dummy variables for the existence of a union, whether all employees were blue collar, whether the firm was in the manufacturing sector, and whether mandatory retirement prior to age 68 was in effect. Regressing plan-level coefficients on these variables, we find that unionized firms have somewhat later retirement ages and blue-collar workers retire significantly earlier. These findings are consistent with nonpecuniary attributes of the job playing a role in determining retirement ages. For instance, unions may increase the attractiveness of the workplace, while blue-collar jobs are less appealing to the older worker. However, early mandatory retirement rules proved to be uncorrelated with retirement patterns, which is consistent with the conclusion that workers react primarily to retirement incomes rather than to mandatory retirement rules.[2] In order to explore these issues in more detail, it would be necessary to obtain better data than available from either the BAS or LRHS surveys; ideally future researchers will have access to firm-level surveys matched with data on workers to pursue these questions in more depth.

3. Evidence on Health and Retirement

Some researchers claim that workers retire because of compulsion rather than choice. In this section we explore the extent to which poor health influences retirement decisions, relative to the economic variables described and derived above.

An analysis of variance (ANOVA) model is used for this purpose. This approach begins by calculating the total variability in the dependent variable as the sum of squared deviations from the mean. In this case the dependent variable is the age of retirement. The total variation is decomposed into two parts: that associated with a set of explanatory variables, called the explained variance, and the remainder that is left unexplained. In turn, the explained variance is decomposed according to groups of explanatory variables. In what follows, the two groups of explanatory variables are economic factors and health.

The two economic variables used are *PDVY60* (the present discounted value of expected lifetime income if the individual retires at age 60) and *YSLOPE* (the gain in present discounted value of expected income if retirement is deferred from age 60 until age 61, 65, or 68). The health variables used reflect health status in 1969, when the workers in the LRHS sample were around age 60. (No health status variables appear in the BAS file.) It is important to use health measures as of the beginning of a decision period since past research suggests that later measures suffer from ex post rationalization.[3] Two alternative measures of 1969 health status are employed here: one indicating whether the individual reports a health limitation but says he can work full time and one that looks at health limitation but ignores the information about ability to work full time.

Table 5.2 presents six alternative ANOVA specifications. All six yield essentially the same results. Consider the first column. The total sum of squares explained is 134.0. Of this, the economic variables explain 102.4 and health just 31.5. Thus three-quarters of what is explained is explained by economic variables. Other specifications appear in columns 2 through 6. The specific numerical values differ, but the preceding conclusion is sustained both qualitatively and quantitatively: economic variables explain most of what can be explained.

4. Summary

Empirical findings using linear regression models estimated on two different data sets strongly support the hypotheses drawn from our theoretical age-of-retirement models. First, economic variables are important determinants of retirement. Second, workers who have more income in some base year retire earlier. Third, workers who expect to gain more income by deferring retirement do postpone retirement. Finally, three-quarters of the explained variance in retirement age is examined by economic factors and only one-quarter by health variables, implying that choice has a large role in the retirement decision.

Our findings also indicate the importance of knowing as much as possible

Table 5.2
Analysis of variance: Sums of squares explained by health and by economic variables, LRHS data

	ANOVA1	ANOVA2	ANOVA3	ANOVA4	ANOVA5	ANOVA6
Health						
Health limitation in 1969 but can work full time	31.5 (.010)		33.3 (.008)	31.9 (.009)		
Health limitation in 1969		41.5 (.003)			43.7 (.002)	42.0 (.003)
Economic variables[a]						
PDVY60 and YSLOPE61			96.7 (.001)		96.7 (.001)	
PDVY60 and YSLOPE65	102.4 (.001)	102.4 (.001)				
PDVY60 and YSLOPE68				99.9 (.001)		99.8 (.001)
Total sum of squares explained	134.0	144.0	130.0	131.8	140.4	141.9

Notes: Dependent variable = age of retirement. Significance levels are in parentheses.
a. PDVY60 is present discounted value of expected lifetime income if the individual retires at age 60. The three YSLOPE variables indicate the gain in present discounted value of expected lifetime income that the individual would realize if he instead retired at age 61, 65, or 68.

about workers' pension plan characteristics in order to explain retirement age patterns in detail. The BAS data file suggests that unionized firms have somewhat later retirement ages, and blue-collar workers retire significantly earlier. This is consistent with nonpecuniary job attributes playing a role in retirement decision making. However, mandatory retirement rules are uncorrelated with retirement ages, which implies that workers react primarily to retirement income streams rather than to mandatory retirement rules.

6   Discrete Choice Models

This chapter probes further into the effects of intertemporal income opportunities on retirement ages. In contrast to the regression model of the last chapter, here we develop a discrete choice framework using the full range of information about workers' budget sets.[1] This is accomplished with two logit models, both of which characterize the decision to retire as a question of selecting from among several different retirement options. In our data sets, the feasible range of alternatives includes all ages between 60 and 68 (or younger if a firm had mandatory retirement prior to age 68). This choice variable is then modeled as a function of the income and leisure available at each retirement age.

The approach developed here is somewhat more general than that of the previous chapter in that the worker's budget set need not be linearized as was necessary for regression equations. In addition, as McFadden (1976) has shown, logit models, unlike the regression equation, are compatible with utility theory. The two logit variants employed here are the more familiar multinomial logit (MNL) and a new extension, termed simple ordered logit (SOL).[2]

1. Retirement in a Discrete Choice Framework

Discrete choice models are designed to handle decision making in cases where the behavior of interest takes on one of several values. Some of the best-known applications of this econometric approach examine the demand for residential housing (McFadden, 1978) and alternative modes of transportation (McFadden, 1979). Studies applying the discrete choice framework to the labor supply context include the work of Heckman (1974) and many others on labor force participation of married women. Amemiya (1981) provides an extensive discussion of many of these models and applications.

It is readily apparent that the dependent variable in the retirement context can be cast in terms of a discrete choice problem: of several different retirement ages, which will the individual select? Frameworks involving dependent variables such as this are usually referred to as polytomous or multiresponse models, of which the logit models detailed in this chapter are one class.

Discrete data analysis has another feature useful for examining retirement behavior: it accommodates nonlinear budget sets without difficulty. As we saw in chapter 3, the budget sets facing older workers are indeed nonlinear. The budget set can be left nonlinear in discrete data analysis, whereas it had to be linearized in the regression model.

A final and extremely important feature of the discrete choice approach is that some forms of it have been shown to be compatible with microeconomic theory. McFadden (1981) shows, for instance, that the multinomial logit model can be derived from utility maximization. This feature of the econometrics of discrete choice is appealing. Of course, the behavioral results from the various approaches can be compared across models; this we do in chapter 8.

2. Specification of the Multinomial and Simple Ordered Logit Models

Because the discrete choice approach posits that utility is derived by selecting one from among many options, modeling this process makes it necessary to compare the utilities of all feasible choices. Estimation in this study employs a function of the Cobb-Douglas type.[3] Here the utility of individual i depends on the present value of the income obtained by retiring at age j, $PDVY_{ij}$, and the leisure available from that particular retirement data, RET_{ij}:

$$U_{ij} = [\alpha \log PDVY_{ij} + \beta \log RET_{ij}] + \varepsilon_{ij}; \quad \alpha > 0, \beta > 0. \tag{6.1}$$

Both α and β are parameters to be estimated using maximum likelihood across the sample of individuals $(i = 1, \ldots, I)$ and across all feasible retirement ages $(j = 1, \ldots, J)$. These parameters indicate the relative weight assigned to income versus leisure by sample members; of special interest here is the null hypothesis that $\alpha = \beta = 0$.

The term in square brackets $[\alpha \log PDVY + \beta \log RET]$ is usually known as the average individual's strict utility associated with specific values of income and leisure. The ith individual's tastes may differ from the average for unobserved reasons, summarized by the disturbance term ε_{ij}, about which additional distributional assumptions are required.[4]

At this juncture two special classes of discrete choice models can be considered: probit and logit. A probit framework maintains that the individual-specific disturbances (ε_{ij}) are distributed multivariate normally across retirement ages for each individual and independently across individuals. Unfortunately the probit likelihood function becomes extremely complex when the number of choices increases and is computationally practical only when the number of options is fewer than five. With nine retirement ages, estimating this function is prohibitively expensive; hence the probit model must be rejected for our application.[5]

The class of discrete choice models in the logit family is a useful alternative. Here individual-specific errors (ε_{ij}) are assumed to be distributed across retirement ages according to a multivariate extreme value or Weibull distribution and independently across individuals. McFadden (1978) shows that the general function:

$$F(\varepsilon_i, \ldots, \varepsilon_J) = \exp\{-G(e^{-\varepsilon_1}, \ldots, e^{-\varepsilon_J})\} \tag{6.2}$$

has a multivariate extreme value distribution; below we present the specific forms of G corresponding to various logit formulations. This gives rise to a probabilistic choice model, which expresses the probability that an individual selects alternative j (P_j) as a function of the characteristics of all J alternatives:

$$P_j = e^{V_j} G_j(e^{V_1}, \ldots, e^{V_J})/G(e^{V_1}, \ldots, e^{V_J}). \tag{6.3}$$

In our specific context, P_j is the probability that retirement age j is selected, and V_j is the strict utility associated with alternative j, the bracketed term in (6.1).

The general class of models given by (6.3) is known as the generalized extreme value (GEV) framework. A simple representative of the GEV class, and the one used most extensively in the applied economics literature, is the MNL model. In our context, this approach expresses the probability that an individual will select retirement age j as follows:

$$P_j = \frac{e^{V_j}}{\sum_{j=1}^{J} e^{V_j}}. \tag{6.4}$$

This corresponds to a specialization of the G function described earlier as:

$$G(y_1, \ldots, y_J) = \sum_{j=1}^{J} y_j, \tag{6.5}$$

where y_j, a function of attributes of retirement age j,[6] is equal to e^{V_j}. An MNL model of the retirement decision is estimated below.

MNL has a shortcoming: it requires that the data conform to a property known as the independence from irrelevant alternatives (IIA). IIA requires that the relative odds for any two choices be independent of the attributes and the availability of any other choices. Although this assumption may be tenable in many behavioral contexts, it seems unnecessarily restrictive for an examination of older individuals. In particular IIA denies the possibility that some workers have strong tastes for income, while others prefer leisure. Rather than imposing IIA, it seems more reasonable to allow some degree of "workaholism" or "leisure loving" and then to test for IIA formally.

One econometric model that permits the testing of IIA is known as ordered logit. This methodology is appropriate when the decision variable can be ordered along a natural dimension. The path-breaking analysis on the model was done by Small (1981, 1982), who examined commuters' decisions to arrive at work early, on time, or late. His problem was similar to the retirement one in several ways: he specified that the decision depended on economic variables, he posited that the choice was based on a comparison of utilities from discrete choices, and his dependent variable (arrival time) was ordered in a temporal way. In addition Small noted that IIA might not hold if, for instance, arriving late is perceived as definitely less satisfactory than arriving early or on time. In other words Small's empirical application, like the retirement problem, was one where a given individual was likely to have an uneven pattern of unobserved tastes across alternatives.

Such a preference structure is appropriate for an SOL model since it maintains that the attractiveness of any given option depends on the attributes of immediately adjacent alternatives, as well as those of the particular alternative in question. In the retirement context, for instance, a workaholic might have a higher probability of remaining at work as long as possible, as compared to his leisure-preferring counterpart who seeks to retire as soon as he can. An SOL model would assign to the workaholic a higher probability than under MNL of choosing the next closest late retirement age; the leisure lover is given a higher probability of choosing the next closest early retirement age. SOL develops a type of autoregressive person-specific taste correlation, thereby tilting the probabilities in one direction or the other as compared with the MNL model.

Such a formulation is made explicit by specifying a G function of the form:

$$G(y_1, \ldots, y_J) = \sum_{j=1}^{J+1} \left(\frac{1}{2} y_j^{1/\rho} + \frac{1}{2} y_{j-1}^{1/\rho} \right)^{\rho}, \tag{6.6}$$

where ρ is an index of adjacent alternatives. Where $\rho = 1$, adjacent alternatives do not affect the choice probabilities directly and IIA holds; when $\rho = 0$, IIA does not hold, and MNL is inappropriate for the empirical problem at hand.

Using (6.3) and (6.6), the probability that an individual selects retirement age j in the SOL context can be written as:

$$P_j = \frac{e^{V_j/\rho}[(e^{V_{j-1}/\rho} + e^{V_j/\rho})^{\rho-1} + (e^{V_j/\rho} + e^{V_{j+1}/\rho})^{\rho-1}]}{\sum_{j=1}^{J+1}(e^{V_j/\rho} + e^{V_{j-1}/\rho})^{\rho}}. \tag{6.7}$$

(Note: For $j = 0$ and $j = J + 1$, take $e^{V_j/\rho} = 0$.) Expression (6.7) requires computationally expensive nonlinear estimation. Therefore Small (1982) proposes approximating (6.7) using a Taylor series expansion about zero, leading to the following simplified expression:

$$P_j \cong \frac{e^{V_j + \sigma N_j}}{\sum_{j=1}^{J} e^{V_j + \sigma N_j}}, \tag{6.8}$$

in which N_j is defined as:

$$N_j = -\tfrac{1}{2}[\log(\tfrac{1}{2}) + \log(1 + P_{j-1}^o/P_j^o) + \log(1 + P_{j+1}^o/P_j^o)] \tag{6.9}$$

and P_k^o is the probability of selecting some other alternative k under the IIA assumption. The variable N_j may be thought of as a proxy for alternative-specific unobserved taste variation, which is omitted in logit models that assume IIA. The accuracy of this approximation is greater when the data more closely fit the IIA property, as Small notes. Future work should evaluate the sensitivity of empirical findings to this approximation and examine model robustness when departures from IIA are severe.

Having constructed an approach that permits but does not require IIA, it is useful to develop statistical tests indicating when MNL would or would not be appropriate. Three different IIA tests are available, although no one of them is universally accepted. The first method, proposed by Hausman and McFadden (1981), compares the estimated coefficient vector using MNL in the full sample with coefficients estimated using a subsample of individuals who elected a subset of the total choice set. The intuition behind this method is that when IIA holds and alternatives are omitted from the data set, behavioral parameters estimated among those who did not elect those choices should be unchanged. The test statistic they develop is:

$$T = (\theta_R - \theta_U)'[\text{cov}(\theta_R) - \text{cov}(\theta_U)]^t(\theta_R - \theta_U) \tag{6.10}$$

where $\theta_U(= (\alpha, \beta)$ from (6.1)) is the coefficient vector estimated for the full sample; θ_R is the coefficient vector estimated using a subset of the total choice set; $\text{cov}(\theta)$ refers to the relevant parameter covariance matrix; and t denotes a generalized inverse. In the present context this test statistic is distributed chi-square with two degrees of freedom[7] and is interpreted such that a value of T

larger than the critical value rejects the independence from irrelevant alternatives assumption for the specific formulation of the model at hand.[8]

Small suggests a second test for IIA, based on the estimated coefficient on N_j in (6.8). N_j proxies alternative-specific variation in tastes; this is present in SOL and absent from MNL. Its coefficient, σ, indicates the importance of such variation. If σ is found to be significantly greater than zero, IIA should be rejected by this test. A negative coefficient would suggest that the specific structure imposed by SOL is, in fact, an inaccurate representation of the data.[9]

A third test of IIA compares the predictions from an MNL and an SOL model, with the presumption that the models will not differ significantly when IIA is roughly correct. In particular, if IIA holds in the data, including the N variable will not alter results substantially; on the other hand when IIA does not hold, SOL predictions will differ from those produced by MNL models. A suitable test statistic is then:

$$V = \sum_{j=1}^{J} \left[\frac{(\hat{P}_j^{SOL} - \hat{P}_j^{MNL})^2}{\hat{P}_j^{MNL}} \right], \tag{6.11}$$

where $\hat{P}_j^{SOL}$ and $\hat{P}_j^{MNL}$ are the predicted frequencies for retirement age j in the SOL and MNL models, respectively. V is distributed chi-square with $J - 1$ degrees of freedom, as discussed in Fields and Mitchell (1984).

In summary, discrete choice models of the logit variety seem well suited to the retirement problem. Both MNL and SOL approaches are estimated empirically in the next section, and tests of IIA follow.

3. Empirical Results

In this section we report and interpret coefficient estimates from both the MNL and the SOL frameworks. In addition we present evidence on the appropriateness of the IIA assumption using the three test statistics proposed. Throughout this section, the goal is to determine how older workers value income relative to leisure—that is, whether α and β are significantly nonzero and whether income or leisure is preferred more strongly in the discrete choice framework. Evidence is provided using both the BAS plan-level sample and the LRHS data set.

BAS Data

Because of the potential for differences in behavior across firms and because early mandatory retirement provisions were in effect in some firms but not others, the ten pension plans in the BAS sample are examined individually rather than in a pooled model. MNL results and SOL coefficient estimates appear in table 6.1.

For all ten plans, the MNL results indicate that both income and leisure are important determinants of retirement ages. Both variables enter the utility functions of older workers, and the null hypotheses that $\alpha = \beta = 0$ are generally rejected: the coefficient on $PDVY$ is significantly greater than zero in all ten plans, and the RET coefficient is significant in eight of ten cases. Therefore, by this model we conclude that economic factors play an important role in determining older workers' retirement patterns.

An examination of the SOL coefficients reiterates the importance of both income and leisure as determinants of retirement. $PDVY$ is statistically non-zero in all ten plans, as before, and RET again is significant in eight of ten. The estimates are similar to MNL findings in some cases; for example, the ratios of α/β and the likelihood ratios are virtually identical.[10] In other cases, however, the results are rather different; for plan 5 the ratio α/β changes by about 18 percent and the log likelihood rises by 16 percent when going to SOL.

It is also interesting to note that the relative weights attached to income and leisure vary across plans. In the SOL columns, for instance, the ratio a/β is two and a half times larger in plan 9 than in plan 3. These findings buttress our evidence from the earlier linear regression models: workers in all firms react to income and leisure opportunities, but they may differ across firms in the ways they react to these opportunities.

In order to judge the performance of the MNL versus the SOL models, it is necessary to test the IIA assumption. We performed the three tests suggested.

Hausman-McFadden Test The calculated values of their suggested T statistics are reported in table 6.2. The T statistics compare the MNL coefficients from the full sample with new coefficients estimated on two subsamples of individuals: those who retired between ages 60 and 65 and those who retired between ages 60 and 62. The calculated values of the test statistic surpass the critical value in all plans for which the test could be performed.[11] This is strong evidence against IIA: tastes for leisure are not uniform in this sample of individuals.

Small's test Looking across the σ coefficients in table 6.1, we note that IIA is rejected in a majority of cases, since eight of ten of the N terms come in with significantly nonzero coefficients. The fact that three values are negative indicates that SOL may not be an exactly appropriate model of unobserved preferences for those plans; in five cases the estimated coefficient is positive as expected.

Chi-Square Test If IIA holds in the data, the predictions from the SOL model will not be identical to the MNL findings. By this test, reported in table 6.2,

Table 6.1
Estimated utility function parameters using alternative logit models, BAS data

Variable	Plan 1 MNL	Plan 1 SOL	Plan 2 MNL	Plan 2 SOL	Plan 3 MNL	Plan 3 SOL	Plan 4 MNL	Plan 4 SOL	Plan 5 MNL	Plan 5 SOL
PDVY (α)	14.15*	14.28*	18.50*	18.92*	12.42*	15.95*	7.98*	8.05*	14.77*	4.97*
	(1.30)	(.45)	(1.50)	(1.55)	(1.01)	(1.15)	(.39)	(.35)	(.85)	(.87)
RET (β)	13.71*	13.85*	16.80*	17.59*	18.65*	25.03*	10.10*	9.63*	15.71*	4.49*
	(1.19)	(1.39)	(1.48)	(1.59)	(1.31)	(1.65)	(.36)	(.37)	(1.00)	(1.00)
N (σ)		−.15		.48		−2.09*		1.65*		6.86*
		(.72)		(.31)		(.30)		(.20)		(.56)
Ln L	−730.35	−730.33	−901.07	−899.88	−1,361.09	−1,336.41	−5,646.51	−5,612.95	−604.92	−507.58
Ratio α/β	.79	1.03	1.03	1.08	1.10	.64	.67	.84	.94	1.11

Variable	Plan 6 MNL	Plan 6 SOL	Plan 7 MNL	Plan 7 SOL	Plan 8 MNL	Plan 8 SOL	Plan 9 MNL	Plan 9 SOL	Plan 10 MNL	Plan 10 SOL
PDVY (α)	0.94*	2.11*	11.85*	8.46*	8.22*	8.63*	21.30*	32.64*	1.23*	3.10*
	(.33)	(.26)	(2.82)	(2.91)	(.64)	(.67)	(3.80)	(6.84)	(.66)	(.61)
RET (β)	−1.09	2.55*	−.65	.67	10.51*	11.12*	14.69*	22.29*	−7.17*	.20
	(.60)	(.69)	(3.12)	(2.99)	(.78)	(.84)	(2.40)	(4.53)	(.90)	(.83)
N (σ)		2.46*		1.37*		−.96*		−1.42*		3.96*
		(.23)		(.50)		(.47)		(.65)		(.21)
Ln L	−1,917.33	−1,863.99	−226.70	−222.84	−1,362.03	−1,359.94	−198.33	−196.06	−1,626.04	−1,438.39
Ratio α/β	n.s.	.95	n.s.	n.s.	.78	.78	1.45	1.46	n.s.	n.s.

Note: Standard errors are in parentheses.
*$t > 1.96$
n.s. = one component not significantly greater than zero.

Table 6.2
Testing IIA with plan-level logit models, BAS data

	Pension Plan Number									
	1	2	3	4	5	6	7	8	9	10
Hausman-McFadden statistics										
T value for subset*										
60 through 65	17.16	23.39	NA	147.32	112.68	NA	NA	183.47	15.24	NA
60 through 62	65.85	63.27	111.99	59.72	141.89	21.09	NA	58.74	NA	33.88
Chi-square statistics										
MNL versus SOL**	691.65	0.60	36.72	52.61	1,217.25	82.33	12.67	1.74	2.19	427.43

*Critical value 10.6 (at $p = .005$).
**Critical value 22.0 (at $p = .005$).
NA = Statistic could not be computed because retirement was mandatory at 65 or no worker chose to retire at 62.

the calculated test statistics surpass the critical values in six of the ten plans. Thus IIA is also rejected in the majority of cases using this third test.

LRHS Data

MNL and SOL coefficients estimated using LRHS data are presented in table 6.3. As before, both models produce estimates for α and β that have the anticipated signs and are significantly greater than zero. Thus both income and leisure enter the utility functions of older workers in the more nationally representative LRHS sample, confirming our results for the BAS data set.

One interesting difference between these results and those presented earlier is that the LRHS ratio of α/β is lower—0.60—than in the BAS pension plans, where the range was from 0.64 to 1.46. This suggests that individuals in the more representative sample seem to place a slightly lower weight on income relative to leisure, as compared to workers covered by the private pension plans for which we have detailed data.

The MNL and SOL coefficients in table 6.3 appear similar. Still, it is worth determining whether IIA holds using the three tests described. For the Hausman-McFadden test, the computed value of their T statistic is 17.22, which surpasses the critical value at the $p = .005$ level (the critical value is 10.60). Thus IIA is rejected by this test. For Small's test, the coefficient is not significantly different from zero. IIA cannot be rejected by Small's suggested formulation. For the chi-square test, in the LRHS data, the chi-square statistic is calculated to equal .528, which is less than the critical value at conventional

Table 6.3
Estimated utility function parameters using alternative logit models, LRHS data

Variable	Method Used	
	MNL	SOL
PDVY (α)	1.46*	1.37*
	(.23)	(.25)
RET (β)	2.43*	2.27*
	(.37)	(.42)
N (σ)		−0.21
		(.27)
Log likelihood	−2,223.56	−2,223.26
Ratio α/β	.60	.60

Note: Standard errors are in parentheses.
* $t > 1.96$

significance levels. IIA cannot be rejected by this test either. Thus in the LRHS data, we reject IIA by the Hausman-McFadden test but do not reject it using the other two criteria.

Given that the estimated coefficients are fairly similar across models, the SOL findings are probably marginally more appealing since IIA is not required in this formation.

4. Summary

This chapter discussed and implemented two discrete choice logit models of the retirement decision. The discrete choice approach has several features in its favor: it is utility based, it is appropriate to empirical settings where observed outcomes take on several distinct values, and it permits the intertemporal budget set to be nonlinear.

For empirical work we posit that the average worker has strict utility of the Cobb-Douglas type; individual-specific taste differences are assumed to be distributed according to a multivariate extreme value or Weibull function. Two particular variants of a logit framework are explored in detail, the multinomial logit and the simple ordered logit models. These are similar in maintaining that utility depends on both leisure and (discounted future) income, but they differ in the way that this dependence is specified. The SOL approach explicitly relaxes the assumption of independence from irrelevant alternatives embodied in MNL. Several tests of IIA are also described.

These two models are estimated using both the BAS and the LRHS data. Empirical results prove to be consistent with theory: economic opportunities influence retirement decisions of older people. These conclusions hold for both data sets. We also find that IIA is clearly rejected using the BAS file, where we have more detail on retirees' incomes. This implies that tastes for leisure are not uniform in the older population represented by the BAS survey. In the LRHS data, IIA is rejected but by only one of the three tests provided. On a priori grounds, the SOL findings are probably to be preferred since that model does not require IIA, and it performs at least as well as the more restrictive alternative. Predictions from these and other models are compared in chapter 8.

7　　A Nonparametric Model

The regression and logit models developed in previous chapters differ in many ways but are similar in one crucial respect: each assumes that individual-specific taste parameters are distributed according to a particular functional form. In the regression case the errors are assumed to be normal, and in the logit case they are assumed to be extreme value or Weibull. This chapter develops a nonparametric approach that does not require individual differences to fit any specific density function. Instead the nonparametric model (NP) uses individual variation in the data to identify utility function parameters directly. This formulation is developed in detail and compared with the more commonly used stochastic models in chapter 8.

1. Model Specification in the Continuous Case

The idea behind the NP model is illustrated with the aid of figure 7.1. Suppose two individuals, A and B, face the same lifetime budget set (for example, because they hold identical jobs). We now observe that worker A retires before worker B; he chooses a longer retirement period (RET) with lower lifetime income (PDVY) than does B. Based on their actions, it is reasonable to infer that A is the leisure lover and B the workaholic. In this way actual choices reveal important information about the two workers' unobserved preferences for income and leisure. In particular, A's indifference curves are revealed to be relatively steep and B's relatively flat; see figure 7.2.

Information revealed by actual choices can be useful for predictive purposes. Consider how individuals A and B might be expected to respond to a particular change in the lifetime budget set, for instance, a given percentage increase in income at each age. Both workers would find themselves richer. Individual A, being a leisure lover, might respond to his increase in wealth by buying additional leisure and retiring even earlier. Individual B, on the other hand, prefers income. The new budget set offers him an even greater gain for

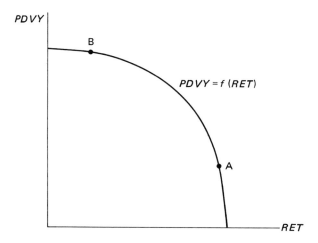

Figure 7.1
Lifetime budget set

postponing retirement. He might therefore be expected to respond to his changed budget set by working still longer. Thus the same change in income opportunities would produce quite different responses from A and B. The NP method is designed to allow for such differential responses when looking across a sample of workers.

The NP method is introduced most readily by first considering the case of a continuously differentiable lifetime budget set. The method will then be modified in order to allow for two special features of our data files: discrete outcomes and kinked budget sets.

As before, let the budget set relationship between present discounted value of lifetime income associated with a particular retirement age for individual i($PDVY_i$) and the corresponding length of retirement period (RET_i) be represented by a function

$$PDVY_i = f_i(RET_i), \tag{7.1}$$

as shown in figure 7.1. When this function is continuously differentiable, the slope of the budget set at any given point is the derivative:

$$\frac{dPDVY_i}{dRET_i} = f_i'. \tag{7.2}$$

Denote the values of $PDVY$ and RET corresponding to individual i's chosen point by $(PDVY_i^*, RET_i^*)$. By revealed preference theory $(PDVY_i^*, RET_i^*)$ is presumed optimal, so that there exists an indifference curve tangent to the

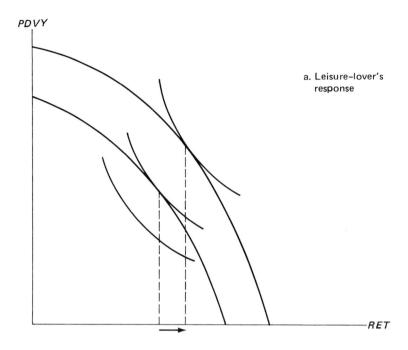

a. Leisure-lover's response

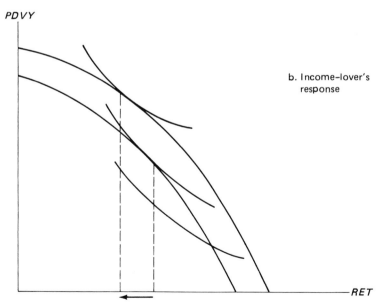

b. Income-lover's response

Figure 7.2
Responses to upward shift in budget set

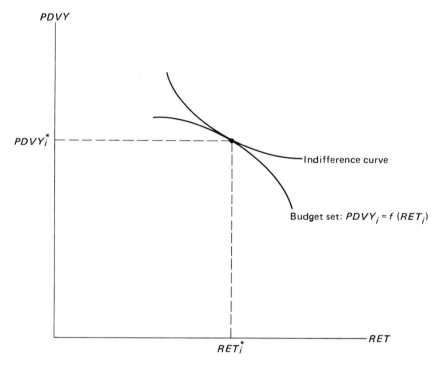

Figure 7.3
Inferring one indifference curve

budget set at that point, as in figure 7.3. The slope of the budget set and the slope of the indifference curve are equal at that point. A sufficient condition for identifying the indifference mapping is that the individual's utility function has a single individual-specific unknown parameter. One such function is a Cobb-Douglas specification (similar to that used in previous chapters):

$$U_i = PDVY_i^{\alpha_i} RET_i^{(1-\alpha_i)}. \tag{7.3}$$

The indifference curve implied by (7.3) has a slope defined by:

$$\frac{dPDVY_i}{dRET_i} = \left(1 - \frac{1}{\alpha_i}\right)\frac{PDVY_i}{RET_i}. \tag{7.4}$$

By revealed preference, (7.2) = (7.4) at the chosen point $(PDVY_i^*, RET_i^*)$:

$$f_i^{*\prime} = \left(1 - \frac{1}{\alpha_i}\right)\frac{PDVY_i^*}{RET_i^*}. \tag{7.5}$$

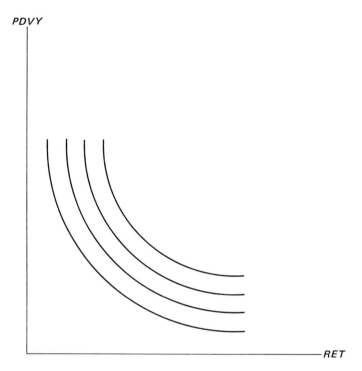

PDVY

RET

Figure 7.4
Indifference Mapping

The only unknown in (7.5) is α_i, which may be solved for as:

$$\alpha_i = 1\Big/\left[1 - \frac{dPDVY_i/PDVY_i}{dRET_i/RET_i}\right].$$
(7.6)

In other words, by knowing which point along the budget set was selected as optimal and the slope of the budget line at that point, we can then identify the single parameter of this Cobb-Douglas utility function. An individual's value of α_i can then be substituted back into equation (7.3) so that any $(PDVY, RET)$ pair can be ranked relative to any other. This permits the completion of the full indifference curve mapping for each person in the sample (figure 7.4).

2. Model Specification in the Discrete Case

Before implementing the NP approach using our data on retirement, two practical problems must be confronted. One is that our data files report the dependent variable (the age of retirement) in whole years only. Consequently instead of determining the effect of a change in the budget constraint by locating a new tangency between the new budget set and an indifference curve, we must instead evaluate each person's utility function at each integer retirement age between 60 and 68 and choose that which generates the highest utility. If people tend to retire near their birthdays, and there is evidence that they do, this not a bad procedure.

The other practical problem is the fact that the budget set is not smooth. This implies that the slope of the budget set is not unique as it appeared in the figures and preceding equations. Therefore we employ two arc slopes, one year to the left and one year to the right of the actual retirement date. The slope of the budget set is then approximated as follows:

$$\frac{dPDVY_i}{dRET_i} = \frac{1}{2}[DIFF_i^+ + DIFF_i^-], \tag{7.7}$$

where $DIFF_i^+ = PDVY_i(RET_i^* + 1) - PDVY_i(RET_i^*)$ and $DIFF_i^- = PDVY_i(RET_i^*) - PDVY_i(RET_i^* - 1)$. Alternatively $DIFF_i^+$ and $DIFF_i^-$ might be used and a range of values computed. In what follows, we work only with (7.7).

3. Empirical Results

In evaluating the empirical results from the NP model, the issue of most interest is the distribution of estimated preferences across individuals. One way to characterize the findings uses the proposition that total utility may be decomposed into two parts, one attributable to income and one attributable to leisure.[1] Then θ_i may be defined as the ratio of utility derived from income divided by total utility, and statistics can be provided about the distribution of this variable in the sample.

For the LRHS data set, the mean value of θ is .42, implying that income contributes about 42 percent of total utility and leisure about 58 percent. This is interpreted to mean that the average individual weighs a given percentage increase in lifetime income less strongly than he would the same percentage increase in leisure years. Across the sample, θ_i has a range from 0 to 1 and is distributed approximately normally, as seen from figure 7.5.[2] For the BAS data set, the mean value of θ is .39, quite close to the .42 value in the LRHS. Again the statistic ranges from 0 to 1.

Putting the results together, older persons appear to value a given percentage increase in leisure relatively more than they would the same percentage increase in income. Additionally the findings indicate that older persons differ greatly among one another in the relative weights they assign to

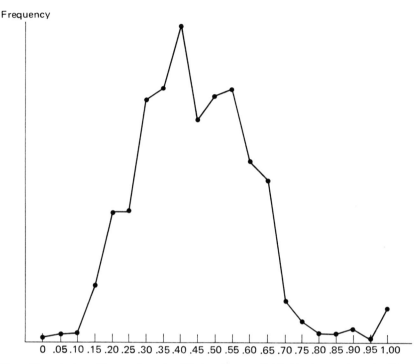

Frequency

0 .05 .10 .15 .20 .25 .30 .35 .40 .45 .50 .55 .60 .65 .70 .75 .80 .85 .90 .95 1.00

Note: Theta is the utility attributed to lifetime income divided by imputed total utility.

Figure 7.5
Distribution of theta: LRHS data

income as opposed to leisure. These findings are used for predictive purposes
in the next chapter.

4. Summary

This chapter developed an alternative method of modeling the determinants
of retirement ages in a discrete choice framework. In contrast to the regression
and logit equations, the NP model does not impose any particular stochastic
assumptions about the distribution of retirees' tastes. Instead observed behavior and data on workers' income and leisure opportunities are used to draw
direct inferences about tastes. Our empirical results show that the average
individual values a percentage increase in income relatively less than he
would the same percentage increase in leisure years during retirement. In
addition there is a great deal of disperson in tastes about the mean, indicating
that older workers differ among themselves in the importance they attach to
income and leisure time away from their jobs.

8 Comparing the Models

1. Evaluating Retirement Age Response to a Change in the Budget Set

Clearly economic factors affect the retirement age decision. This key result is robust across all model specifications and data sets. Thus the qualitative conclusion is not at issue. What remains to be examined in this chapter is whether the various models yield different predictions about the signs and magnitudes of the responses to economic factors. This chapter poses and answers the question: Do the regression, logit, and nonparametric models provide different estimates of retirement age responses to economic variables?

To arrive at a judgment, a standard for comparison is required. The coefficients from the various models are not directly comparable. Instead we perform a hypothetical experiment and evaluate predicted retirement responses across the several empirical formulations. The particular counterfactual evaluated here is that of a 10 percent reduction in Social Security benefits available at each possible retirement age.[1] This exercise then asks (1) by how much older individuals would defer retirement if faced with such a benefit cut and (2) whether the various empirical frameworks used here yield consistent predictions across data sets.

Budget sets for each of the ten BAS pension plans appear in summary form in table 8.1. (All data in this chapter are in 1970 dollars.) Experimentally lowering benefits by 10 percent has two effects on the pattern of intertemporal income opportunities for older workers: it lowers income at each possible retirement age, and it also lowers the amount of additional income gained by a worker who defers retirement. The behavioral effect of lower income at each age should be to induce workers to remain on their jobs longer, thus increasing the retirement age. Lowering the reward to deferring retirement has both income and substitution effects; the income effect will encourage prolonged work, and the substitution effect would make leisure more attractive since its opportunity cost is now relatively less. It is anticipated that the net effect will

Table 8.1
Lifetime budget set prior to and after a 10 percent reduction in Social Security Benefits, plan-level BAS data

| | | Retirement Age: | | | | | | | | |
		60	61	62	63	64	65	66	67	68
Present discounted value of Social Security benefits										
Plan 1	Actual[a]	$28,589	$29,529	$30,412	$31,930	$33,304	$34,332	$33,203	$31,947	$30,561
	Experimental[b]	25,730	26,576	27,370	28,737	29,974	30,899	29,883	28,752	27,505
Plan 2	Actual	28,688	29,750	30,731	32,348	33,810	34,928	33,831		
	Experimental	25,819	26,775	27,658	29,113	30,429	31,435	30,448		
Plan 3	Actual	28,786	29,761	30,697	32,230	33,618	34,670			
	Experimental	25,907	26,785	27,627	29,007	30,256	31,203			
Plan 4	Actual	28,895	29,844	30,750	32,289	33,681	34,728	33,584	32,300	30,863
	Experimental	26,006	26,860	27,675	29,060	30,313	31,256	30,226	29,070	27,777
Plan 5	Actual	27,187	28,081	28,869	30,229	31,456	32,378	31,252	29,998	28,626
	Experimental	24,468	25,273	25,982	27,206	28,310	29,140	28,127	26,998	25,763
Plan 6	Actual	28,530	29,555	30,479	32,010	33,393	34,432			
	Experimental	25,677	26,560	27,431	28,809	30,054	30,989			
Plan 7	Actual	26,635	27,743	28,821	30,523	32,078	33,338			
	Experimental	23,972	24,969	25,939	27,471	28,870	30,004			
Plan 8	Actual	29,264	30,159	31,057	32,616	34,035	35,087	33,948	32,643	31,193
	Experimental	26,338	27,143	27,951	29,354	30,632	31,578	30,553	29,379	28,074
Plan 9	Actual	28,432	29,411	30,294	31,842	33,245	34,357	33,255	32,005	30,610
	Experimental	25,589	26,470	27,265	28,658	29,921	30,921	29,930	28,805	27,549
Plan 10	Actual	28,616	29,558	30,443	31,958	33,337	34,395			
	Experimental	25,754	26,602	27,399	28,762	30,003	30,956			

Present discounted value of lifetime income

Plan 1	Actual	57,468	64,977	72,370	78,845	84,923	90,592	94,586	98,028	100,968
	Experimental	54,609	62,023	69,328	75,652	81,593	87,159	91,265	94,833	97,912
Plan 2	Actual	63,888	72,099	80,298	88,689	96,493	103,580	107,992		
	Experimental	61,019	68,925	77,225	85,453	93,112	100,087	104,609		
Plan 3	Actual	62,381	70,023	77,785	84,313	90,535	96,288			
	Experimental	59,502	67,047	74,715	81,090	87,174	92,821			
Plan 4	Actual	59,285	67,041	75,057	82,171	88,885	95,132	99,679	103,605	106,974
	Experimental	56,396	64,057	71,977	78,942	85,517	91,660	96,321	100,375	103,887
Plan 5	Actual	27,187	33,484	40,599	48,086	55,308	64,733	67,887	70,165	71,955
	Experimental	24,468	30,676	36,812	45,063	52,163	61,494	64,762	67,164	69,091
Plan 6	Actual	39,469	48,789	62,629	70,189	77,251	83,547			
	Experimental	36,616	45,795	59,582	66,987	73,912	80,105			
Plan 7	Actual	49,018	58,842	68,179	77,781	87,043	95,366			
	Experimental	46,355	56,069	65,287	74,729	83,836	92,033			
Plan 8	Actual	59,885	71,738	82,555	91,985	100,864	109,163	114,189	118,401	121,906
	Experimental	56,959	68,722	79,449	88,723	97,462	105,654	110,795	115,136	118,787
Plan 9	Actual	46,088	53,593	61,239	69,631	78,340	86,750	91,735	96,546	100,779
	Experimental	43,244	50,652	58,210	66,447	75,015	83,314	88,411	93,347	97,718
Plan 10	Actual	47,872	55,112	62,091	70,921	79,294	86,833			
	Experimental	45,010	52,156	59,047	67,725	75,960	83,394			

Note: Empty cells cannot be computed because of mandatory retirement rules at that age in that firm.
a. At the time the BAS workers were making retirement decisions.
b. If Social Security benefits were lowered by 10 percent.

be to induce workers to defer retirement, so that on average, retirement ages would be expected to rise.

Table 8.2 presents a similar set of figures for the LRHS sample, again indicating the present value of Social Security payments before and after the experimental reduction in benefits. Here too the experiment reduces workers' total incomes regardless of when they retire; in addition, those who defer retirement to older ages are rewarded by smaller dollar amounts. Since the overall pattern of changes in the LRHS lifetime budget set is similar to that discerned for the BAS sample workers, we anticipate that on average these changes will induce workers to defer retirement, just as in the case of the BAS workers.

The reduction in benefits means more in dollar terms in the LRHS budget sets as compared to the BAS, since in the former, wives' benefits were included in Social Security computations but could not be computed for the latter.

2. Predicted Responses: Regression Results

It is straightforward to use the regression results from chapter 5 to predict changes in retirement ages in response to the 10 percent reduction in Social Security benefits. We focus here on the equation using $PDVY60$ and $YSLOPE65$, though models using other measures of the change in income from deferring retirement would produce similar results.

To predict a change in retirement ages given the BAS experimental budget sets in table 8.1, we compute how $PDVY60$ and $YSLOPE$ change (in thousands of dollars) and apply these figures to the regression estimates appearing in column 1 of table 5.1:

$$\Delta\, RETAGE = -\,0.039\, \Delta\, PDVY60 + 0.030\, \Delta\, YSLOPE65, \tag{8.1}$$

where Δ refers to the change in the variable in moving from the actual to the experimental budget set. Solving for the appropriate values, we find for the first of the ten plans:

$$\Delta\, RETAGE = -0.039(-2.859) + 0.030(-0.574)$$
$$= +0.09 \text{ years, or } +1.1 \text{ months.} \tag{8.2}$$

Substitution of changes in $PDVY60$ and $YSLOPE65$ for the other plans yields similar results, on the order of 1.0 to 1.2 months, with an average of 1.1 months. Thus using the regression model on the BAS data, a 10 percent decrease in Social Security benefits is estimated to increase the average retirement age by about 1.1 months.

Table 8.2
Lifetime budget set prior to and after a 10 percent reduction in Social Security Benefits, LRHS data

	Retirement Age								
	60	61	62	63	64	65	66	67	68
Present discounted value of social security benefits									
Actual[a]	$31,727	$33,029	$34,514	$38,417	$42,389	$46,230	$48,046	$49,610	$50,904
Experimental[b]	28,554	29,726	31,063	34,575	38,150	41,607	43,241	44,649	45,814
Present discounted value of lifetime income									
Actual	34,802	43,359	52,498	64,023	73,719	83,184	90,432	96,501	101,905
Experimental	31,629	40,056	49,047	60,181	69,480	78,556	85,627	91,540	96,815

a. At the time the LRHS workers were making retirement decisions.
b. If Social Security benefits were lowered by 10 percent.

To predict a change in retirement ages for the LRHS data, we compute the resultant changes in *PDVY60* and *YSLOPE* for table 8.2 and apply these changes to the change form of equation (5.2):

$$RETAGE = -0.031(-3.173) + 0.007(-4.838)$$
$$= +0.07 \text{ years,} \quad \text{or } +0.9 \text{ months.} \tag{8.3}$$

Thus the regression model used with LRHS data indicates that a 10 percent decrease in Social Security benefits is estimated to increase the average retirement age by about 0.9 months.

3. Predicted Responses: Multinomial Logit Results

In order to predict the change in retirement patterns using the multinomial logit framework, we combine the MNL coefficients derived in chapter 6 with the income profile incorporating the changed Social Security benefit stream to predict the probability of retirement at each age between 60 and 68. Having determined these new retirement age probabilities for each person, we then sum the probabilities across the entire sample and compare them with the initial retirement age patterns. Estimated changes in retirement age probabilities are then weighted by the relevant age to derive the mean change in retirement age. We find that a 10 percent decrease in Social Security benefits would increase the average retirement age by about 0.6 months in the BAS data; in the LRHS sample the figure is 0.5 months.

4. Predicted Responses: Simple Ordered Logit Results

Predictions using the SOL model devised in a manner analogous to that described in section 3 except that the SOL coefficients from chapter 6 were used instead of the MNL estimates. The SOL coefficients indicate that a 10 percent decrease in Social Security benefits would lead to an increase in the average retirement age of about 0.8 months in the BAS data; the figure for the LRHS sample is 0.5 months.

5. Predicted Responses: Nonparametric Results

Finally, we may evaluate how the ith individual would be expected to alter his retirement age in response to the specified change in his budget set using the nonparametric model of chapter 7. A reduction in Social Security benefits at each age would lower the lifetime budget set from $f(\cdot)$ to $g(\cdot)$ in figure 8.1. The

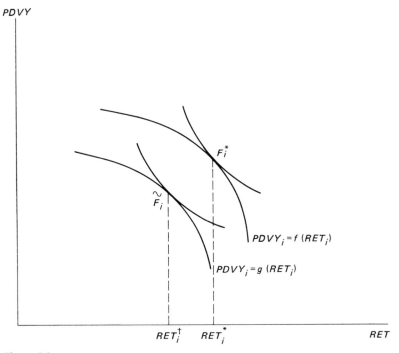

Figure 8.1
Effect of change in budget set on retirement age using NP method

highest indifference curve was originally tangent at F_i^*. With the new budget set, the tangency is at $\tilde{F}_i$, and the optimal retirement age is $RET_i^\dagger$. This is readily found using the NP method by substituting all $(PDVY_i, RET_i)$ pairs from the new budget constraint $g(\cdot)$ into (7.3) and (7.6) and finding the pair that yields the highest utility. The change in retirement age due to the specified change in the budget set is $R_i = RET_i^* - RET_i^\dagger$. Responses are then summed across all individuals in the sample and divided by the sample and divided by the sample size to obtain the average change in retirement age.

Using the estimated distribution of α_i derived in chapter 7, we conclude that a 10 percent decrease in Social Security benefits would increase the average retirement age by about 1.7 months in the LRHS and by 0.7 months in the BAS.

6. Comparing the Predictions

In table 8.3 we collect the predictions derived from the four models and two data files examined in this chapter. Plan-by-plan results for the BAS data appear in table 8.4. Several conclusions emerge.

Table 8.3

Effect of a 10 percent reduction in Social Security Benefits: Predicted changes in average retirement age

Model Specification	Predicted Change in Average Retirement Age (in months)	
	BAS[a]	LRHS
Linear regression	+1.1	+0.9
Multinomial logit	+0.6	+0.5
Simple ordered logit	+0.8	+0.5
Nonparametric	+0.7	+1.7

[a]Ten-plan average; individual plan results appear in table 8.4.

First, all of the models are in complete agreement with regard to their qualitative predictions. In each case the results indicate that people would work longer in response to a cut in Social Security benefits. This unanimity across models and data sets is important because it indicates our findings are robust to the way in which observed tastes are modeled.

Second, the models are in substantial agreement with respect to their quantitative findings. In particular a 10 percent change in retirement benefits is predicted to have an extremely small impact on retirement ages—on the order of one month or so.

Third, to the extent that the models' predictions do differ, there appears to be no systematic pattern across econometric methods. In one data set the linear regression model produces the largest behavioral responses, but in another the NP model generates the biggest predicted changes. The two logit models give rise to virtually identical quantitative estimates. The observed similarity is especially interesting in the BAS, in which IIA was rejected in the majority of pension plans. It seems to make little difference whether unobserved tastes are assumed to vary normally, Weibull, or nonparametrically in our data sets.

7. Summary

This chapter evaluated four econometric models of retirement using the BAS and the LRHS. Predicted retirement age responses were compared using a hypothetical experiment—a 10 percent reduction in Social Security benefits. Looking across models, there is substantial agreement about the signs and the magnitudes of responses to this hypothetical change in older workers' budget sets. On average a decrease in Social Security benefits of this magnitude would

Table 8.4
Effect of a 10 percent reduction in social security benefits: Predicted changes in average retirement age in months for plan-level BAS data

Model Specification	Plan Number										Ten-Plan Average
	1	2	3	4	5	6	7	8	9	10	
Regression	+1.1	+1.1	+1.1	+1.2	+1.1	+1.1	+1.0	+1.2	+1.1	+1.1	+1.1
Multinomial logit	+0.2	+0.7	+0.6	+0.7	+1.2	+0.1	+0.1	+0.7	+1.2	+0.1	+0.6
Ordered logit	+0.8	+0.7	+0.5	+0.8	+1.7	+0.5	+0.2	+0.7	+1.2	+0.4	+0.8
Nonparametric	+0.4	+0.2	+1.7	+0.2	+0.8	+0.2	+0.4	+0.4	+1.7	+1.2	+0.7

be predicted to have an extremely small supply-side effect—an increase of one month. In general it seems to make little difference whether unobserved tastes are assumed to be distributed normally, Weibull, or allowed to vary nonparametrically.

IV

Applications

Previous chapters estimated four behavioral models of the economic determinants of retirement behavior. This part uses some of these behavioral estimates to examine two empirical phenomena: different retirement ages in different firms and retirement age responses to Social Security reforms.

Chapter 9 investigates differences in average retirement ages across pension plans. These differences are found to be associated systematically with the behavioral parameters discerned in part III, reflecting differences in worker preferences for income and leisure across firms. Average retirement ages also prove to be correlated with the pension structures themselves, in that people retire later in firms offering the greatest financial incentives to remain on the job. Finally, our evidence also suggests some degree of association across pension plans between average worker preferences and the economic incentives for retirement.

In chapter 10 we use the logit models of part III to predict how workers reaching retirement age during the 1980s might be expected to respond to reforms in the Social Security system. The four reforms examined here are increasing the normal retirement age, delaying the cost-of-living adjustment, raising the late retirement credit, and changing the early retirement reduction factor. All four policy reforms are predicted to increase the average retirement age by only a small amount. In consequence, the reforms are predicted to lower retirees' incomes.

9   Why Do Retirement Ages Differ across Pension Plans?

Throughout part III the empirical goal was to determine how individual workers would alter retirement behavior if presented with exogenous changes in the income opportunities they faced. In this sense those chapters focused on retirement age differences across individual workers. In this chapter we step back in order to consider and explain differences in retirement pattern across pension plans. Previous studies have not examined this issue since other data sets do not contain plan identifiers as in the BAS.

That retirement ages do differ across pension plans is evident from table 9.1; the overall retirement age for the individuals from the ten plans is 63.7, but plan-specific averages range from 61.8 to 65.7. Several economic explanations are possible: either the economic incentives for retirement differ systematically across plans, or workers' preferences for income and leisure may vary systematically across plans, or both explanations may hold. Determining which explanations fit the data is the goal of this chapter.

1. Retirement Ages and Worker Preferences

In order to see if retirement ages and worker tastes for income and leisure are associated across plans, it is first necessary to devise a summary measure for worker preferences. The analysis in chapter 6 used logit models to produce plan-specific estimates of the weights workers attached to income (α) and leisure (β). A natural summary statistic is therefore the ratio α/β, indicating how strongly a group of workers prefers additional income to additional leisure.

Table 9.2 collects α/β estimates from chapter 6 for all plans where the underlying ordered logit coefficients were statistically significant. It is evident that this ratio covaries with retirement age exactly. It attains its maximum ($\alpha/\beta = 1.5$) for the plan where retirement occurred latest and falls almost monotonically down to the plan with the earliest retirement age (where

Table 9.1
Average Retirement ages by plan, BAS data

Plan Number	Mean Retirement Age in Years $(\bar{R})$
1	63.27
2	63.53
3	61.82
4	62.77
5	64.67
6	63.18
7	64.71
8	63.17
9	65.69
10	64.17
Overall mean	63.70

Table 9.2
Retirement ages $(\bar{R})$, preferences (α/β), and income opportunities (PDVY60 and YSLOPE in thousands of dollars) in ten pension plans, BAS data

Plan Number	$\bar{R}$	α/β	PDVY60	YSLOPE65
9	65.69	1.46	46.1	40.7
7	64.71	n.s.	49.0	46.3
5	64.67	1.11	27.2	37.5
10	64.17	n.s.	47.8	39.0
2	63.53	1.08	63.9	39.7
1	63.27	1.03	57.5	33.1
6	63.18	.95	39.5	44.1
8	63.17	.78	59.9	49.2
4	62.77	.84	59.3	35.8
3	61.82	.64	62.4	33.9

n.s. = Logit results not significant.

Table 9.3
Rankings of average retirement age ($\bar{R}$) and preference for income over leisure (α/β), BAS data

Rank (Highest to Lowest)	$\bar{R}$	α/β
1	Plan 9	Plan 9
2	5	5
3	2	2
4	1	1
5	6	6
6	8	4
7	4	8
8	3	3

$\alpha/\beta = 0.6$). Evidently, workers retire earlier in plans where average preferences for income are relatively less; where workers value income more, they also retire later. Ranks appear in table 9.3. The simple rank-order correlation coefficient is .98; the conventional correlation coefficient of $\bar{R}$ with α/β is .94.

In sum, those plans that have later average retirement ages are the plans in which workers have stronger average relative preferences for income versus leisure.

2. Retirement Ages and Income Opportunities

Economic incentives clearly play a role in explaining individual differences in retirement at the microlevel. We now investigate whether average retirement ages at the plan level are also responsive in this way. In particular, it is of interest to inquire whether plans offering more income on early retirement in fact have earlier average retirement ages (holding constant the rewards for deferring retirement) and whether plans offering a greater reward for postponing retirement have higher average retirement ages (for a given early retirement benefit).

Operationalizing these notions requires examining the last two columns of table 9.2, which contain plan-level values of two variables reflecting these income opportunities. *PDVY60* measures the present discounted value of net income if the worker retires at age 60; *YSLOPE65* represents the change in the present value of income if retirement is deferred until age 65. (Both variables are measured in thousands of dollars.)

Comparing these income measures with $\bar{R}$, it is evident that they are correlated, albeit imperfectly. The simple correlation between $\bar{R}$ and *PDVY60* is . -59, and between $\bar{R}$ and *YSLOPE* it is .32. The association of retirement ages with each income measure in turn is only slightly different; the partial correlation of $\bar{R}$ with *PDVY60* is $-.58$ and .30 with *YSLOPE*. Therefore some of the variation in retirement ages across plans is attributable to differences in income opportunities available to workers in the plans, though not as much as was attributable to differences in worker preferences.

It is useful to identify more clearly the source of this income variability across plans by recalling tables 3.3, 3.4, and 3.5. These summarized the net present values of earnings, private pension benefits, and Social Security income for alternative retirement ages in each plan. That evidence suggested that PDVYs vary across plans primarily because of differences in private pension benefit structures rather than because of differences in other components of the intertemporal budget set. Combined with the correlation evidence in this chapter, we conclude that retirement ages respond to income variations across plans largely because of the differences in private pension structures.

3. Is There Sorting?

Firms and workers may sort themselves according to their respective preferences for continued work. Firms differ according to the productivity value of additional seniority. In some industries such as heavy manufacturing, older workers may be less productive per dollar spent than are younger workers. Such firms would be expected to create incentives for older workers to leave at relatively young ages. One way to do this is to provide larger retirement income benefits for those workers who retire early. If workers are aware of the differential incentives offered by different employers, individuals with relatively high preference for leisure as compared to income would be more likely to seek employment in firms offering higher early retirement benefits. Empirically this leads us to expect that our measure of the strength of workers' preferences for income versus leisure (α/β) would be negatively associated with income on early retirement $(PDVY60)$. The simple correlation between α/β and *PDVY60* is $-.45$ and the partial correlation controlling for *YSLOPE* is $-.47$. This suggests that sorting does take place.

4. Summary

This chapter attempted to explain differences in retirement ages across the sample of ten pension plans for which we have developed reliable information on key variables. Before concluding that these findings are robust, it would be useful to extend the analysis beyond our relatively small sample of pension plans. Nonetheless our results are quite clear-cut.

Differences in retirement ages across plans can be explained both by differences in workers' tastes and by differences in the economic rewards for retirement embedded in individual pension plans. Specifically, plans with later-than-average retirement ages are those in which workers have a stronger average relative preference for income versus leisure; plans with later-than-average retirement ages are also those with larger than average economic incentives to remain on the job.

Differences in worker tastes appear to be more strongly associated with retirement patterns than are differences in incentives across plans.

There appears to be some evidence of workers with lower tastes for income sorting themselves into pension plans providing higher-than-average benefits for early retirement.

In this chapter we use the models we have developed to predict how older workers reaching retirement age during the 1980s might be expected to respond to reforms in Social Security benefit formulas. Estimates of how their retirement incomes would be affected are also provided. The four reforms simulated are similar to those enacted by Congress in the spring of 1983 or proposed earlier by the Reagan administration: increasing the normal retirement age, delaying the cost-of-living adjustment, raising the late retirement credit, and changing the early retirement reduction factor.

Five steps are required in order to evaluate the likely effects of these reforms:

1. Constructing the intertemporal budget set confronting individuals nearing retirement age.

2. Evaluating how each Social Security reform would alter the budget set.

3. Inferring tastes for income and leisure among older people by examining the behavior of a group of workers now fully retired.

4. Using the budget sets and taste parameters from the first three steps to predict how older workers might alter their retirement ages if Social Security were restructured.

5. Using the changes in rules and retirement ages to compute changes in retirees' incomes after the reforms are implemented.

1. The Intertemporal Budget Set in 1982

The baseline date for the calculations in this chapter is 1982, prior to the Social Security reforms of 1983.[1] In order to evaluate retirement responses to changes in intertemporal budget sets due to 1983 reforms, it is necessary to establish the intertemporal budget set in 1982. Unfortunately there are no data sets such as the BAS or the LRHS that can be used to determine income streams and retirement patterns for such recent cohorts. Therefore we are required to build on the budget set information devised in part II, updated appropriately.[2]

Since 1970 nominal wages increased greatly, Accordingly gross earnings for older workers in the LRHS were adjusted upward by assuming that economy-wide wage growth would have applied equally to older workers. Income taxes and Social Security taxes were then netted out using 1982 formulas.

Private pension benefits had also increased over the years, at least in nominal terms. Benefit amounts derived for the LRHS sample in the 1970s were updated by computing their value in 1982 dollars assuming no real growth. Since the earlier figures had benefits falling in real terms after the retiree left his main job, so too do the updated pension quantities. Net real benefits were obtained by reducing all benefits by the 1982 income tax. Present values were figured as before, adjusting for a 2 percent real discount rate and mortality probabilities.

Social Security benefits had increased in real terms until .1977 due to inadvertent double indexing. Once this was corrected, real Social Security benefits rose only in proportion to increases in the consumer price index. As with private pensions, nominal benefits were assumed to increase with inflation; thus real benefits were held constant. Social Security rules in 1982 are used in the calculations here.[3]

The components of the 1982 budget set thus constructed are presented in table 10.1. The figures given there are for an illustrative worker, the average individual from the LRHS with earnings, pension, and Social Security benefits updated to 1982. For retirement ages 60 and 61, we assume that the individual files for Social Security benefits as soon as he is eligible—at age 62. For other ages benefits are calculated assuming that he files for Social Security in the year he retires. Furthermore, if he is married, his wife is assumed to file for spouse's benefits when he does or, if she is not yet eligible, at age 62.

The first three rows of table 10.1 show annual real earnings, real private pension benefits, and real Social Security benefits, all expressed in 1982 dollars. The next three rows give the corresponding present discounted values, calculated as before on the assumption of a 2 percent real discount rate and the most recent available survival probabilities. The resultant present discounted value of income from earnings, private pensions, and Social Security together appears in the last row.

The microdata summarized in the table are used in three ways: they are compared with income values under the several Social Security reforms discussed, they are used to derive predicted retirement ages from the existing

Table 10.1
Components of 1982 pre-reform budget set for LRHS illustrative worker (1982 dollars)

	Retirement Age								
	60	61	62	63	64	65	66	67	68
Annual amounts									
(1) Net earnings	$16,424	$16,265	$16,330	$16,012	$15,882	$15,952	$15,877	$15,845	$15,752
(2) Net private pension benefits	837	962	1,356	1,875	1,817	1,896	2,128	2,129	2,069
(3) Social Security benefit: Husband	5,378	5,401	5,456	5,964	6,481	7,017	7,307	7,605	7,610
Wife	2,549	2,579	2,636	2,720	2,823	2,948	3,069	3,190	3,301
Present discounted values									
(4) PDVE	0	15,793	30,803	45,238	58,770	71,580	83,836	95,432	106,406
(5) PDVPP	4,272	4,697	6,315	8,318	7,657	7,573	8,036	7,575	6,914
(5) PDVSS: Husband	67,402	67,697	68,387	69,242	69,515	69,341	66,311	63,173	59,928
Wife	25,126	25,245	25,482	25,696	25,836	25,819	25,429	24,782	23,842
Total lifetime income[a]									
[PDVY = (4) + (5) + (6)]	96,800	113,433	130,988	148,495	161,790	174,315	183,613	190,963	197,092

Note: Computations use 1982 Social Security rules.
a. Totals may differ from column sums due to rounding.

budget set, and they are employed to predict changes in retirement ages from changes in the budget set.

2. Changes in the Intertemporal Budget Set under Various Social Security Reforms

Before we can explain how the various Social Security reforms would be expected to change Social Security benefits and hence the intertemporal budget set, some explanation is needed on how Social Security benefits are determined.

The first step in calculating Social Security benefits is to find the worker's average indexed monthly earnings (AIME). The AIME is found by indexing earnings up to the Social Security taxable maximum in each year between 1951 and age 60; comparing these to nominal earnings, if any, after that age; selecting the highest (for example, a worker turning age 60 in 1982 would have his highest twenty-eight years of earnings included); and averaging.

The second step in calculating Social Security benefits is to determine the workers' primary insurance amount (PIA). In 1982, PIA was determined from AIME according to the following formula:

90% of AIME up to "BEND POINT 1"

plus

32% of AIME between "BEND POINT 1" and "BEND POINT 2"

plus

15% of AIME above "BEND POINT 2."

In real 1982 dollars, "BEND POINT 1" = \$230 and "BEND POINT 2" = \$1,388; in future years, the bend points will increase with the consumer price index, thus remaining the same in real terms.

The third step is to compute the worker's Social Security benefit as a multiple of the PIA: Worker's benefit = PIA * multiple. This multiple equals 1.00 if the worker is age 65 when he begins to collect benefits; this is the age of retirement from the point of the view of the Social Security system. Early retirement reduction factors are applied to workers commencing benefits before age 65, and delayed retirement credits are awarded to workers waiting until after age 65 to retire. The multiples for retirement ages other than 65 are determined from these early retirement reduction factors and delayed retirement credits.

The final step is to add in spouse's benefits, if any. The wife is eligible to receive benefits based on the worker's PIA. At age 65 she receives a benefit equal to 50 percent of her husband's PIA, regardless of whether he retired at age 65, earlier, or later. If the wife is 62 or over but not yet 65, she may receive a reduced benefit; the reduction is at the rate of $8\frac{1}{3}$ percent per year.

Various Social Security reforms operate primarily by affecting the multiples. The 1982 rules and the reforms simulated are explained with the aid of figure 10.1. The 1982 rules appear in the top panel. For ease of comparison, they are redrawn in each of the remaining panels.

Under the 1982 rules the early retirement reduction factor was $6\frac{2}{3}$ percent per year and the delayed retirement credit 3 percent per year, both figured to the nearest month. A worker retiring at age 62 would receive a Social Security benefit that is 20 percent less than his PIA ($6\frac{2}{3}$ percent reduction per year times three years under age 65); his multiple at age 62 is thus 0.80. If that same worker waited to retire until age 68, he would receive a Social Security benefit 9 percent greater than his PIA (3 percent credit per year times three years); his multiple at age 68 is thus 1.09.

Four Social Security reforms are simulated.

Experiment A: Increasing the Normal Retirement Age The individual no longer receives his full PIA if he retires at age 65. We simulated the effect of raising this age to age 68, as was widely proposed. (What in fact was legislated was a change to age 66 by the year 2009 and to age 67 by the year 2027.) Under the simulated reform, the multiple becomes 1.00 at age 68, and the early retirement reduction factor remains at $6\frac{2}{3}$ percent per year. Thus the multiples under this experiment are 0.60 for retirement at age 62 and 0.80 for retirement at age 65, with corresponding reductions at other ages. (The 1983 legislation set a minimum multiple of 70 percent.)

Experiment B: Delaying the Cost-of-Living Adjustment Rules in effect in 1982 specified that cost-of-living adjustments would take place each July 1, reflecting increases in the consumer price index during the preceding calendar year. The 1983 Social Security amendments delayed these increases by an additional six months. This six-month delay reduces real benefits by half the rate of inflation, or 2.3 percent. This reduction imposes new multiples as shown in figure 10.1.

Experiment C: Raising the Late Retirement Credit Benefits are increased faster than 3 percent if retirement is postponed beyond age 65. We simulated a $6\frac{2}{3}$ percent per year late retirement credit, the same as the early retirement reduction factor. The multiple for retirement at age 68 would have risen from 1.09 to 1.20. (As it turned out, in 1983 Congress mandated a gradual increase in the late retirement credit, eventually reaching 8 percent per year as of the year 2009.)

Experiment D: Changing the Early Retirement Reduction Factor This experi-

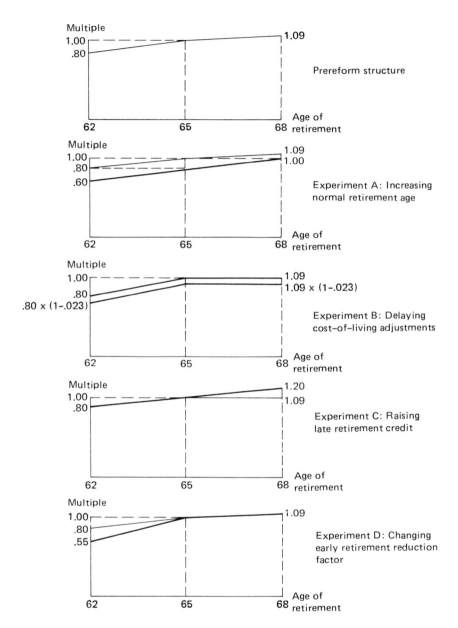

Figure 10.1
Restructuring Social Security benefits: Four experiments

ment simulates a proposal tentatively put forth by the Reagan administration in 1981: to reduce early benefits by 15 percent per year rather than by $6\frac{2}{3}$ percent. The multiple for retirement at age 62 would therefore have been 0.55 rather than 0.80 as at present. This proposal was quickly rejected as politically unpopular and has not yet been resurrected. Still it is interesting to predict what might have happened had it been enacted.

Table 10.2 presents the effects of these four policy experiments on the Social Security benefits of the illustrative LRHS worker, and table 10.3 reports their effects on total income (PDVY). In these computations the earnings and private pension elements of the underlying budget set are assumed to be unaffected by the simulated changes in Social Security structures. Hence the estimated impacts of the various reforms on retirement ages should be thought of as partial equilibrium estimates, leaving aside possible responses of pension plans and earnings profiles to changes in Social Security.

Increasing the normal retirement age to 68 (experiment A) lowers retirement benefits substantially. Annual payments fall by $1,000 or more regardless of when the worker retires. This translates into PDV streams that are lower by about $17,000 for people retiring in their early 60s; the reduction is only somewhat smaller for workers deferring retirement until age 65. Another effect of experiment A is to tilt the Social Security benefit structure. The system becomes actuarially more advantageous until age 65, such that delaying retirement from age 62 to age 65 increases the present value of benefits by some $4,000. The experimental benefit structure is also roughly neutral after age 65, in stark contrast to the prereform penalty. In overview, then, increasing the normal retirement age as outlined here lowers benefits at any given retirement age and provides new financial incentives to remain on the job longer.

Experiment B, in which the cost-of-living adjustment has been postponed six months, has a relatively small effect. Annual benefits are reduced by $100 to $200, which translates into falls in present discounted values of at most $1,600. Since the income amounts involved are small, this reform does not appreciably alter the pattern of discounted benefit gains obtained by deferring retirement.

Experiment C raises the late retirement credit to match the early retirement reduction factor. Benefits are increased after age 65, raising annual benefits by as much as $800 at age 68. Present value at age 68 increases by $6,000—still not enough to achieve actuarial neutrality but substantially reducing the penalty (in PDV terms) for continuing to work beyond age 65.

Experiment D would have lowered early Social Security benefits, holding benefits beyond age 65 the same. For a worker retiring at age 62 or before, the

Table 10.2
Effects of the experiments on annual and present discounted values of Social Security benefits for illustrative worker (1982 dollars)

	Retirement Age								
	60[a]	61[a]	62	63	64	65	66	67	68
Annual Social Security benefits									
Status quo	$5,378	$5,401	$5,456	$5,964	$6,481	$7,017	$7,307	$7,605	$7,910
Experiment A	4,034	4,052	4,093	4,588	5,092	5,614	6,148	6,696	7,256
Experiment B	5,255	5,278	5,331	5,827	6,332	6,856	7,139	7,430	7,728
Experiment C	5,378	5,401	5,456	5,964	6,481	7,017	7,567	8,131	8,707
Experiment D	3,698	3,714	3,752	4,818	5,903	7,017	7,307	7,605	7,910
PDV of Social Security benefits									
Status quo	67,402	67,796	68,387	69,242	69,515	69,341	66,311	63,173	59,928
Experiment A	50,566	50,783	51,300	53,275	54,624	55,474	55,798	55,621	54,974
Experiment B	65,852	66,140	66,814	67,649	67,916	67,746	64,786	61,720	58,550
Experiment C	67,402	67,697	68,387	69,242	69,515	69,342	68,674	67,540	65,969
Experiment D	46,352	46,551	47,025	55,936	63,316	69,342	66,311	63,173	59,928

Note: Figures reported are husbands' benefits. Wives' benefits remain constant since they are calculated from their husband's PIA, which does not change in these experiments.

a. These are the benefits the illustrative individual would receive if he filed for benefits at age 62 but retired at the age indicated.

Table 10.3

Effects of experiments on the present value of total lifetime income

	Retirement Age								
	60	61	62	63	64	65	66	67	68
Current system	$96,801	$113,433	$130,988	$148,495	$161,780	$174,315	$183,613	$190,963	$197,092
Experiment A: Increasing normal retirement age	77,964	96,519	113,900	132,528	146,888	160,447	173,100	183,411	192,138
Experiment B: Delaying cost-of-living adjustments	95,251	111,870	129,415	146,902	160,181	172,720	182,088	189,510	195,714
Experiment C: Raising late retirement credit	96,801	113,433	130,988	148,495	161,780	174,315	185,976	195,330	203,132
Experiment D: Changing early retirement reduction factor	75,750	92,287	109,625	135,189	155,580	174,315	183,613	190,963	197,092

annual benefit would have fallen by $1,700 and present discounted value by some $21,000. The gain in present discounted value of Social Security benefits for an extra year of work before age 65 would have been $6,000 to $9,000. This reform would have created a powerful penalty for retiring early and a powerful incentive for continued work. Yet even these forces would not change retirement ages very much.

3. Preferences for Income and Leisure

Part III estimated four behavioral models. The logit models are most appealing a priori because they allow the greatest flexibility in specifying nonlinearities in the intertemporal budget set while retaining a utility-based framework. Within the logit class, the SOL model offers the advantage of permitting but not maintaining IIA. By contrast, MNL requires IIA. These considerations lead us to prefer the SOL specification and to use that model for the four Social Security reform simulations.

4. Effects on Retirement Ages

To predict the effects of the four experiments on retirement ages, we first use the SOL coefficients to predict for all sample individuals the probability that each alternative retirement age will be chosen under the prereform budget set. Then we predict retirement ages under all four experimental budget sets. Finally we average over individuals. The results appear in the first column of table 10.4.

We find that the estimated retirement age responses vary depending on the experiment performed.[4] The largest retirement age response is observed for the experiment that cuts benefits at the earliest retirement age while offering a larger reward to continued work before age 65 (experiment D). The likely response to this reform would be on average about a three-month delay in the retirement age. Intermediate retirement responses are observed for the experiment that lowers benefits by approximately the same dollar amount at every age but leaves unchanged the incentive to remain working an additional year. This is accomplished by changing the normal retirement age (experiment A). This would be predicted to delay retirement by about one and a half months, on average. The smallest responses are obtained in cases where income incentives for early retirement are altered the least. This is true for delaying cost-of-living adjustments (experiment B), in which benefits at each retirement age are reduced somewhat. It is also true of the experiment to raise the late retirement credit (experiment C) since early retirement benefits are

Table 10.4
Effects of experiments on retirement ages and present discounted values of Social Security benefits (PDVSS) and total lifetime income (PDVY)

	Change in Retirement Age in Months ($\Delta \bar{R}$)	Effect on Social Security Benefits		Effect on Total Lifetime Income	
		% Δ PDVSS at Mean Retirement Age	% Δ PDVSS with Retirement Age Endogenous	% Δ PDVY at Mean Retirement Age	% Δ PDVY with Retirement Age Endogenous
Experiment A: Increasing normal retirement age	+1.6	−22	−22	−10	−9
Experiment B: Delaying cost-of-living adjustments	+0.1	−2	−2	−1	−1
Experiment C: Raising late retirement credit	+0.2	0	0	0	0
Experiment D: Changing early retirement reduction factor	+2.9	−13	−11	−6	−3

unaffected and most workers retire prior to age 65. Each of these reforms would be predicted to delay retirement by less than a week on average. Overall the four policies simulated here generate only very small changes in retirement behavior; changes of lifetime income of as much as 20 to 30 percent at some ages would result in at most a three-month deferral.

It is useful to compare and contrast our findings with others in the literature. First, the major point of similarity is that our findings are very much like those generated from other recent models of the effects of Social Security reform on older workers' labor supply. Burtless and Moffitt's (1982) results are of the same order of magnitude as ours; their model indicates that changing Social Security benefits by 10 percent would affect retirement ages by about one month. Hausman and Wise (1983) evaluate a slightly different reform; they assess how retirement ages would differ if Social Security PIAs had remained constant from 1969 onward instead of increasing as they did until 1975. This counterfactual simulation indicates that retirement at age 62 would not have been affected at all; only 3 percent fewer people would have retired at age 65 and about 4 percent fewer at age 66. Since the actual PIA increase was on the order of 50 percent over that period, these estimated responses prove to be quite small indeed. Finally, Gustman and Steinmeier (1983b) estimate the effects of raising the normal retirement age for Social Security benefits from 65 to 67. This reduces early benefits by ten to thirteen and one-third percentage points in each year. They estimate that the two-year increase in the normal retirement age would increase actual retirement by about two months; this is somewhat larger than our prediction that a three-year increase in the normal retirement age would increase actual retirement by about 1.6 months, but both are very small. They also find as we do that the cost-of-living adjustment deferral is expected to raise actual retirement by less than one month. In sum the numbers that emerge from our study are very close to others' estimates. We all find very small elasticities of retirement age with respect to changes in Social Security benefits: on the order of 0.1 or less.

The major point of contrast is that these behavioral estimates are an order of magnitude smaller than actuarial assumptions made in many Social Security simulations. Schieber (1982, pp. 188–190) is particularly clear on the assumptions being made by Social Security actuaries: "These simulations *assumed* that there would be a behavioral response as a result of the increased Social Security normal retirement age. . . . The increases in the statutory retirement ages, however, were greater than the increases in the actual retirement ages that were simulated here, corresponding with the Social Security actuaries' *assumptions* regarding the potential response to this option. . . . In this simulation [in which the normal retirement age is raised from 65 to 68] the average age at retirement for men is *assumed* to rise to 65.5 years at the end of the transition, which contrasts with an average retirement age of 63.2 years at the beginning of the simulation" [emphasis added]. Thus the Social Security actuaries were assuming a 2.3-year response to a three-year increase in the normal retirement age. The behavioral evidence we and others find suggests that this assumption is unwarranted; the probable response is no more than a tenth of that.

The small retirement age responses predicted from behavioral models have implications for the financial viability of the Social Security system and of workers. First, looking at the Social Security system, the average worker is predicted to make only a marginal change in response to a downward shift in benefit formulas. This means that the Social Security system will have to pay out less to the worker over his lifetime. Furthermore, during the weeks or months of extra work, the system gains additional revenues. The system therefore comes out ahead from these reforms.

Does the financial gain to the Social Security system necessarily imply a corresponding financial loss to Social Security recipients? Not necessarily, if workers respond as the actuaries assume and extend their work lives by enough to retain their old benefit levels; however, the behavioral evidence from several models, including ours, suggests otherwise: older workers will not give up much leisure. Consequently the models predict that workers will be rendered poorer. We turn now to estimates of the changes in incomes of retirees.

5. Effects on Retirement Incomes

Table 10.4 also indicates how each of the four experiments would alter a retiree's Social Security benefits (PDVSS) and total income (PDVY). Two sets of calculations are presented: one assumes the worker is employed until the average retirement age prior to the reforms, and the other allows the retirement age to respond to benefit changes.

At the mean retirement age we find that the present value of Social Security benefits would be reduced by as much as 22 percent. The largest reduction in PDVSS occurs in experiment A, which increases the normal retirement age, leaves the early retirement age unchanged, and maintains the gain for working an extra year (hereafter, the "tilt") at $6\frac{2}{3}$ percent per annum.

At the mean retirement age, the present value of remaining lifetime income would be reduced by as much as 10 percent. Once again the largest reduction is found for experiment A. The PDVY reductions are smaller than the corresponding PDVSS reductions because PDVSS is just one component of PDVY.

After allowing for the average retirement age to respond to changes in the Social Security benefit structure, PDVSS would still fall by as much as 22 percent and PDVY by 9 percent under experiment A. The effects are largest under this experiment for two reasons: experiment A reduces benefits at the mean by nearly as much as experiment D, much more than any other experiment, and experiment A leaves unchanged the prereform tilt, thus providing a smaller incentive for prolonged work than under some other experiments.

For the experiment that lowers early retirement benefits while keeping normal benefits the same (experiment C), the percentage reduction in PDVY is less after allowing for retirement age endogeneity than when retirement ages are held constant. This experiment increases the tilt in the benefit structure, as well as reducing Social Security benefits at any given age. The consequent labor supply response would offset about half of the lifetime income reduction that would otherwise take place.

In the other experiments retirement ages do not change appreciably, so the effects on PDVSS and PDVY are the same when the retirement age is allowed to vary as when it is taken as exogenously determined.

6. Summary

This chapter has evaluated the likely responses of older workers to four reforms in the Social Security benefit formulas: increasing the normal retirement age, delaying the cost-of-living adjustment, raising the late retirement credit, and changing the early retirement reduction factor. This process first required developing workers' intertemporal budget sets prior to and after the reforms. Next it was necessary to evaluate how retirement behavior might respond to these new economic incentives. Estimated taste parameters from a previous chapter were employed for this purpose. Finally, new retirement ages and retirement incomes were compared with prereform levels.

We find that the estimated retirement age responses depend on the policy reform in question. The largest response is observed for the experiment that cuts benefits at the earliest ages, while offering larger rewards to continued work. The likely response for this change would be about a three-month delay in the average retirement age. An intermediate change—about one and a half months—was predicted in response to increasing the normal retirement age. Very small responses—less than one week—were obtained for delays in the cost-of-living adjustment or raising the late retirement credit, both of which altered income incentives the least.

Responses of these magnitudes would be too small to compensate retirees for reductions in benefit formulas. Thus smaller Social Security benefits would be paid to workers. The Social Security system's financial burden would be eased, but retirees' incomes would fall on average.

V   Conclusion

The overview we present here proceeds in four steps. First, the analytical framework is reviewed, along with a restatement of our economic approach to the retirement problem. Next we collect key lessons about older workers' intertemporal budget sets derived using the BAS and LRHS surveys. This is followed by a set of conclusions drawn from the four empirical models used to evaluate how economic factors affect retirement decisions. Applications and policy implications complete the discussion.

Lessons and Implications

At the outset, this book posed two empirical questions: (1) What are the income opportunities facing older workers at all retirement ages? (2) How responsive are older workers' retirement ages to changes in income opportunities? In this chapter we collect answers to these questions as reported in parts I to IV. Two important policy questions are also examined: the anticipated effects of Social Security reforms on retirement ages and retirement incomes and the likely impact of mandating private pension neutrality.

1. The Analytical Framework

The Importance of Economic Factors as Determinants of Retirement

One view of retirement is that it is compelled by poor health, mandatory retirement provisions in firms, or by other noneconomic factors. An alternative view is that retirement is a matter of choice in which the decision maker weighs the leisure gained by retiring at a given age against the income forgone by not working. Evidence from other studies and new results presented here suggest that choices based on economic factors are of primary importance for most older workers; health and other noneconomic factors matter too, but they matter less.

More workers have better retirement income opportunities available to them than ever before. These enhanced income opportunities enable workers to retire earlier. Evidence on retirement patterns through time indicates that people are taking advantage of these opportunities. Older workers have not been forced to retire earlier; they have chosen to do so.

Thinking about Retirement in an Economic Framework

Our theoretical approach to modeling retirement behavior began by recognizing that retirement is an intertemporal, or life-cycle, decision. In other words choosing when to retire requires that the worker decide whether to work (or how much work to do) in each of many periods.

The economic variables explaining retirement are intertemporal as well: economic opportunities in the past, present, and future are needed to understand the choice of retirement date. In particular, streams of net earnings, private pension benefits, and Social Security income for each alternative retirement age must be evaluated. The joint consideration of all these factors for each possible retirement age, though a central feature of theoretical retirement models, receives its first empirical implementation in this book.

Our age-of-retirement model generated several interesting findings. The optimal retirement date is one at which the worker equates the marginal utility of income gained by additional work with the marginal disutility of forgone income and leisure. It was also proved that the higher a worker's base pension, the earlier he will retire (other things constant). However, changes in earnings streams or pension accrual rates have an ambiguous impact on the optimal age of retirement.

2. Empirical Findings: The Intertemporal Budget Set

Our examination of the intertemporal income opportunities available to older workers was guided by two questions: (1) What would a typical worker retiring at age 60 anticipate receiving in earnings, private pension, and Social Security benefits? (2) How would these income streams change if he were to defer retirement?

Two data sets were used to address these questions: the LHRS and the Labour Department's BAS. For the average worker retirement at age 60 would have generated an income stream of about $35,000 in the LRHS data and about $51,000 in the BAS (in 1970 dollars). These two amounts differ mainly because the BAS sample was limited to workers covered by private pensions.

An examination of income patterns at other retirement ages also suggests some interesting findings:

1. Private pensions vary widely in the way they reward deferred retirement. In some plans the present value of expected net pension benefits increased in real terms if a worker deferred retirement. In other plans benefits would have fallen if the worker had waited to retire.

2. The present value of Social Security benefits would have been expected to increase if retirement were postponed, for both data sets examined.

3. On average the older worker in both data files would have always added to his income by deferring retirement.

4. The expected gains to deferring retirement, though always positive, were not uniform; work paid more than twice as much at some ages than at others.

An in-depth analysis of the structures of fourteen pension plans using the BAS data revealed a host of interesting details not evident in other, less informative data sets. In particular we found that the two types of defined benefit pension plans examined here differ in their overall incentive structures. Pattern plans (those based on years of service only) appeared to encourage early retirement as a rule, while conventional plans (those that use final salary as well as years of service) tended to reward later retirement. The BAS data also indicated a great deal of cross-plan variability in the way benefits are structured. These patterns were linked to employee behavior.

3. Empirical Findings: Behavioral Models

Regression Models

Theory led us to hypothesize that the age of retirement could be modeled as a negative function of *PDVY60* (the private pension plus Social Security wealth an individual would receive if he retired at an early baseline age, which we took to be age 60) and a positive function of *YSLOPE* (the anticipated gain in the present value of lifetime income if the individual retired later than this baseline age). Our empirical findings, estimated on both the BAS and LRHS data sets, were supportive of the theoretical hypotheses. First, economic variables were important determinants of retirement ages. Second, workers with more base year pension and Social Security wealth did retire earlier. Third, those who expected to gain more income by deferring retirement did postpone retiring. Finally, three-quarters of the explained variance in retirement patterns was attributable to economic factors and only one-quarter to health variables. These facts together imply that choice, rather than compulsion, plays a significant role in the retirement decision, in ways consistent with economic theory.

Our findings also indicated the importance of knowing the detailed rules determining pension benefits and Social Security options. Previous studies generally have not included as explanatory variables income values at future retirement ages; yet this proves to be important in our work. In addition the BAS data set suggested that nonpecuniary job attributes may also play a role in retirement. Ideally future researchers will have access to firm-level surveys matched with data on workers and will be able to pursue these issues further.

Discrete Choice Models

A discrete choice framework has several features that make it appropriate to the retirement problem: it is utility based, it can handle cases where observed outcomes take on distinct values, and it readily accommodates intertemporal budget sets, which are nonlinear. In our empirical analysis of retirement, we posited that workers have a strict utility function of the Cobb-Douglas type. Individual-specific taste differences were also allowed and were assumed to be distributed according to the Weibull function. Two different models were explored, MNL and SOL. These were similar in that both assume that older workers derive utility from both leisure and future income flows but differ from one another in the particular way this dependence was specified. The SOL approach explicitly relaxed a central assumption in the MNL model, that of IIA. Several tests of IIA were also described.

The MNL and SOL models were estimated using both the BAS and the LRHS data sets. Empirical results again were consistent with theory in that economic opportunities did appear to influence retirement decisions of older people. These conclusions held for both data sets. We also noted that IIA was rejected using the BAS workers, where more detail was given on retirees' income streams. This implies that tastes for leisure were not uniform in the older population. Using the LRHS data, IIA was rejected by only one of the tests proposed. Overall SOL was to be preferred on theoretical grounds since it did not require IIA and performed at least as well as MNL.

A Nonparametric Model

An alternative method of modeling the determinants of retirement ages was developed; in contrast to the regression and logit models, it did not require that older workers' tastes for income versus leisure be distributed in any particular way, Instead data on workers' income opportunities were combined with observed retirement behavior to infer what each worker's tastes for income and leisure must have been. A great deal of dispersion in tastes was found. On average, however, older workers were found to weigh a percentage increase in income less than they would the same percentage increase in years of retirement.

Comparing the Models

How similar or different are the predictions of the four models estimated on two different data sets? Because the coefficients of the various models are not directly comparable, we compared them by asking how responsive retirement ages are to a specified change in the intertemporal budget set. The hypothetical experiment examined was that of a 10 percent reduction in Social Security benefits at each age.

One important conclusion was that all of the models are in complete agreement with regard to their qualitative predictions. The findings all indicate that people would work longer in response to this benefit cut. The unanimity across models and data sets indicates that our findings are robust to the way in which unobserved tastes are modeled. The consistency of our results stands in marked contrast to previous studies, which have provided conflicting and ambiguous results on the effects of Social Security on retirement.

A second conclusion was that in all the models, this 10 percent benefit reduction is predicted to have an extremely small impact on retirement ages —on the order of only a month or so. It seems to make little difference whether unobserved tastes were assumed to vary normally, Weibull, or nonparametrically.

Next, there appeared to be no systematic pattern across economic models in that different models produced different rankings in the two data sets. However, the two logit models gave rise to virtually identical estimates, which is interesting given that they make different assumptions about the underlying pattern of tastes (and that IIA was rejected in a majority of cases).

Another conclusion was that the dispersion of results across models was slightly larger in the LRHS than in the BAS. This may be a reflection of the greater sample variability in that data file as compared to the BAS.

In overview, all four models provided the same answer for both data sets: people would have deferred retirement by only a small amount if Social Security benefits had been reduced.

4. Applications and Policy Implications

Differences in Retirement Patterns across Pension Plans

Previous chapters sought to determine why individual workers selected different retirement ages. Using the BAS data set, it was also possible to attempt to explain differences in retirement ages across pension plans. Previous studies have not examined this issue since other data sets do not contain plan identifiers as in the BAS.

Our analysis showed that workers in different firms did retire at quite different ages, on average. We found:

1. Differences in retirement ages across plans can be explained both by differences in workers' tastes and by differences in the economic rewards for retirement.

2. Plans with later-than-average retirement ages have workers who on average have stronger relative preferences for income versus leisure.

3. Plans with later-than-average retirement ages offer above-average economic rewards for remaining on the job.

4. Differences in retirement patterns appear to be more strongly associated with differences in worker tastes than with differences in economic incentives.

5. Some evidence was found for worker sorting, that is, those who prefer leisure sort themselves into pension plans providing higher-than-average benefits for early retirement.

These differences across pension plans help assess an idea recently heard in policy circles—that the federal government should mandate private pension benefit neutrality. This proposal is motivated by the belief that pension structures currently encourage early retirement. It is thought that mandatory pension neutrality would result in higher benefits for those continuing to work beyond age 60, thereby encouraging longer work-force commitment. Our analysis, however, shows that the actual result depends on the benefit structure currently available to the covered employee. In pattern plans the effect of mandatory neutrality probably would be to cut early benefits rather than to increase later ones. Although this would affect retirement ages in the anticipated direction, retirement benefits would be lower than at present, not higher. In conventional plans, on the other hand, mandatory neutrality conceivably could remove the desired incentives currently in place to defer retirement; such a result would not be consistent with federal efforts to encourage later retirement. Altering pension reward structures currently in place could produce other undesirable results as well. If the current pension benefit patterns are structured in accordance with firms' perceptions of the relative efficiency of older workers compared to younger ones, imposing regulatory restrictions would be expected to increase firms' costs, some part of which probably would be passed on to workers in the form of lower wages or lower pension benefits, or both. Both the welfare and the efficiency costs of mandating pension neutrality should be analyzed much more carefully before concluding that such a policy is desirable.

Reforming Social Security

Another highly policy-relevant application of our retirement model was to evaluate the likely effects of Social Security reforms. We simulated several reforms similar to those legislated in 1983 or proposed previously. This required developing workers' prereform and postreform intertemporal budget sets and evaluating how retirement behavior and retirement incomes would be likely to change in response to these new economic incentives. Behavioral coefficients from the SOL model and updated LRHS budget sets were employed for this purpose.

Under all four policy experiments, older people ended up with lower incomes during their retirement years. This occurred because all of the proposals reduced benefits and workers would not delay retirement by enough to regain either their previous level of Social Security payments or their previous income from earnings and pensions combined. In particular, raising the normal retirement age and delaying the cost-of-living adjustment would induce older workers to defer retirement, but by only one or two months. Responses of this magnitude are insufficient to compensate retirees for benefit reductions.

In general our estimates of retirement age responses are very close to those from other recent studies on older workers' labor supply, despite important differences in methodology and data definitions. These findings contradict the much larger changes to retirement ages assumed by policy analysts and actuaries who do not use a labor supply approach. Actuarial projections of alternative policy scenarios should build in behavioral estimates of the correct magnitudes in order to predict better the financial viability of the Social Security system.

It should also be recalled that the elderly differ among themselves in their abilities and inclinations to respond to new economic circumstances. Two groups that we have not examined here are likely to have even less hope for altering their labor supply: the sick and the unemployed. These people will be among those hardest hit by benefit cuts, despite being the least able to bear the burden. Their needs should not be forgotten.

A Final Word

The demographic trend is clear: the age composition of the U.S. population of the twenty-first century will resemble that of the population of the state of Florida today. Consequently retirement ages and retirement incomes will grow in importance in policy discussions. Economic analysis of the type we have presented in this book is essential to a well-informed debate.

Notes

Introduction

1. Note to British readers: In American English, the term *Social Security* refers to state pensions and the term *private pensions* to occupational pensions.

2. Of course, noneconomic factors matter too, but they are not our primary concern here. Good places to begin to get into the noneconomics literature are the works of Sheppard and Rix (1977) and Gordus (1981).

Chapter 1

1. A similar pattern is reported by Gustman and Steinmeier (1983a) using the Longitudinal Retirement History Survey data.

2. In fact as disability benefits have become more available over time, male labor force participation rates have fallen (Lando, Coate, and Kraus, 1979; Leonard, 1979).

3. How to measure health—by self-reporting, physician examination, days spent in hospital, medical expenses, or some other measure—is a controversial issue.

4. For instance, Parsons (1982) reports that the mortality rate for males aged 45–54 fell by almost 20 percent between 1956 and 1976.

5. Social Security is financed by a payroll tax. The amount of earnings subject to the tax—the Social Security taxable maximum—has increased over the years. In 1984 it is $37,800. In the future it will increase each year with economy-wide wage increases the year before. Earnings up to the taxable maximum are taxed at the rate of 7.0 percent. By contrast, the taxable maximum was $3,000 in 1937; the tax rate then was 1 percent.

6. The data in this paragraph are taken from Upp (1983). They are based on the March 1981 Current Population Survey, covering income in 1980. See also Schulz (1980) and Schieber (1982).

7. Before proceeding to discuss private pensions, it is useful to clarify terminology. Sometimes the term *private pensions* is used to refer to pensions provided by employers, in contrast to Social Security pensions, which are provided by government. The term *employer-provided pensions* would provide a clear contrast, but this is such a mouthful that *private pensions* is used instead. Other times *private pensions* is used to

denote pensions provided to persons who retire from private firms, as distinct from government employee pensions. Similarly the term *government pensions* is used ambiguously, usually referring to government employee pensions but sometimes referring to all pensions provided by the public sector, including Social Security. Throughout this book we use *private pensions* in the first sense—as a shorthand for employer-provided pensions. We will not have occasion to use the term *government pensions* again.

8. The data in this paragraph are from Munnell (1982) and Ippolito (1983).

Chapter 2

1. These theoretical studies permit private pensions and Social Security benefits to be actuarially unfair; the extra benefit the individual receives by working another year does not necessarily equal the value of his or her contributions to the pension fund in that year. Earlier studies developed predictions about the effects of pensions on retirement assuming actuarial fairness throughout; examples are Feldstein (1977), Sheshinski (1978), and Kotlikoff (1979). Because Social Security and private pension structures confronting our sample workers are in fact not actuarially neutral, this theoretical discussion focuses only on such nonneutral structures.

2. Cf. the treatment of part-time work in the life-cycle models of Reimers (1977), Clark and Johnson (1980), Heckman and MaCurdy (1980), Sammartino (1980), Gustman and Steinmeier (1984), and Burtless and Moffitt (1982)—all of which were developed primarily for empirical purposes—and in the earlier non–life-cycle models of Boskin and Hurd (1978) and Zabalza, Pissarides, and Barton (1980). This assumption also reflects empirical reality. Most individuals never work after accepting a pension. For the BAS sample described in this book, this proportion is 72 percent.

3. Theoretical and empirical studies on retirement through 1982 are reviewed in Mitchell and Fields (1982) and Lazear (1983).

4. Because additional work never lowers future years' benefits.

6. We assume individuals plan to consume all of their income or leave it as a bequest before they die, so income may be substituted in the utility function in place of consumption.

7. For an elaboration of these comparative statics, see Fields and Mitchell (1984).

8. In this model $\partial C_i / \partial PDVY_i = 1$.

9. Diamond and Hausman (1984, pp. 107–8) arrive at a similar conclusion: "Thus at any point in time the individual presumably solves the choice problem which arises from the complicated stochastic dynamic program of whether or not to retire. Formulation and the solution of such a problem is well beyond the scope of the current research."

Chapter 3

1. Among the users of the LRHS are Boskin and Hurd (1978), Burkhauser and Quinn (1980), Burtless and Moffitt (1982), Clark and Johnson (1980), Gordon and Blinder

(1980), Gustman and Steinmeier (1984), Hamermesh (1982), Hausman and Wise (1983), Hurd and Boskin (1981), Quinn (1977), and Sammartino (1980). For an overview of the data base and findings from it, see Schwab and Irelan (1981).

2. A defined benefit pension plan is one in which the pension amount is determined as a function of years of service, final year's or years' salary, or some combination of these. By contrast, a defined contribution pension plan is one in which the pension amount is a function of prior pension contributions and age. We excluded defined contribution plans because the BAS file contained no information on pension contributions. Our data file contained no information on funding of defined benefit pension plans. For an analysis of that issue, see Barnow and Ehrenberg (1979).

3. The present values appearing in row 2 of table 3.1 are not directly comparable to those reported in Blinder, Gordon, and Wise (1980, 1981) or Burkhauser and Turner (1981). Our calculations embody forward-looking expectational assumptions taking 1970 as the decision date. In other words, we projected what a 60-year-old man in 1970 might have expected to receive if he retired immediately, if he retired at age 61, 62, and so on up to age 68. Throughout, the income stream is forecast from past experience, recognizing that Social Security benefits had increased in real terms during the 1960s and that benefit increases were in place for 1972. Previous authors have not done this.

4. We can tell that marital status is responsible by observing Social Security benefits at age 65. If the worker retires at that age, his wife receives a spouse's benefit approximately equal to 50 percent of his benefit. (Her benefit is exactly 50 percent of his if she also is 65 years old and somewhat less than 50 percent if she is younger than he.) Suppose then that the average BAS worker was married, as most men that age are. The combined worker and spouse's benefit would be $51,398—about 10 percent higher than the corresponding figure in the LRHS ($46,230) and just in line with the earnings differences between the two samples.

Chapter 4

1. This chapter draws on a discussion appearing in Mitchell and Fields (forthcoming).

2. Some pension plans offer a joint and survivor option, where a worker's pension is reduced so that if he dies first, his widow receives a pension for as long as she lives. The joint and survivor option has the same actuarial value as the individual option, so for our purposes, it does not matter which is chosen.

3. If there was no mandatory retirement age in the firm, we used age 68 as the latest year for which benefits were computed. In practice, few people worked as late as this age, suggesting that age truncation is not a serious matter for the time period of interest.

4. Because several plans had mandatory retirement after age 65, plan averages could not be computed for retirement past that point. Individual plan-specific patterns are discussed below, including benefits for later retirement ages where permitted.

5. One methodological difference between Lazear's work and ours is that our data set contained information on the actual earnings of workers covered by the pension plans under study. In contrast, Lazear used hypothetical earnings profiles for benefit computations.

Chapter 5

1. Sensitivity analysis using data from a single pension plan reveals that alternative formulations affect the results very little (see Fields and Mitchell, 1985). For instance, using the gain in income from age 60 to 68 instead of the income change between age 60 and 65 produces identical qualitative and almost identical quantitative findings. In general, all models employing *PDVY* and *YSLOPE* types of variables generate negative income effects and (implied) positive substitution effects, consistent with theory. In contrast, additive models frequently found in the literature, which enter earnings, pension, and Social Security variables separately, do not produce such consistent findings. For instance, in our earlier work, we found that the additively separable models sometimes suggest that higher pensions induce labor force withdrawal but higher Social Security payments would encourage continued work. It appears that models incorporating the interactions inherent in the lifetime budget set produce estimates more internally consistent and more compatible with theory, as compared to the ad hoc regressions that enter income components separately.

2. Burkhauser and Quinn (1983) arrive at a similar conclusion.

3. See, for instance, Bazzoli (1983), Parsons (1982), and Anderson and Burkhauser (1983).

Chapter 6

1. A more detailed discussion of discrete choice models in the retirement context appears in Mitchell and Fields (1984).

2. Despite its name, simple ordered logit is not simple. It generalizes the MNL model by incorporating the utilities of nearby alternatives. It may also be extended further; see Small (1981).

3. In a related model, Gustman and Steinmeier (1983a) find an elasticity of substitution between income and leisure of 0.9 for older individuals, so that the Cobb-Douglas model, which assumes an elasticity of 1.0, is probably quite accurate.

4. Thus both the regression and the discrete choice models are stochastic since both require distributional assumptions about person-specific unobserved variability. An alternative approach is discussed in chapter 7.

5. Hausman and Wise (1978) discuss size limitations in multioutcome probit models. Three-state probit models of retirement probabilities have been estimated by Boskin and Hurd (1978), Zabalza, Pissarides, and Barton (1980), and Burtless and Hausman (1982), among others. In their models the dependent variable is the choice at a given time among full retirement, partial retirement, and full work. To our knowledge no one has used a probit model to examine intertemporal labor supply and the choice between a number of alternative retirement ages (in our case, nine).

6. In the MNL model equation (6.4), the individual's enjoyment of one specific retirement age is not directly affected by the attributes of some other age; rather the characteristics of other alternatives enter in computing the relative appeal of all

alternatives, in the denominator of the P_j expression. This formulation is most directly linked with utility theory and is often called conditional logit (Amemiya, 1981). It may be contrasted with universal logit in which attributes of all states are postulated to enter the P_j ratio in the numerator as well as the denominator.

7. The relevant degrees of freedom are given by $df = tr\{[\text{cov}(\theta_R) - \text{cov}(\theta_U)]^t[\text{cov}(\theta_R) - \text{cov}(\theta_U)]\}$.

8. Hausman and McFadden (1981) make the point that alternative specifications of explanatory variables might satisfy the IIA assumption, as might alternative functional relationships.

9. For instance, the SOL model required that the data not deviate too much from IIA; a negative coefficient on N may be an indication that departures from IIA are serious. Additionally Small's approximation formula for the SOL model uses a Taylor series expansion about zero, which may or may not be appropriate to the data. More research on this point is necessary; suffice it to say that a negative coefficient on N is not compatible theoretically with the underlying model, though the data are not constrained to produce positve values. In fact Small's own empirical results indicate that negative values of σ are rather common in practice.

10. Only the ratios of coefficients, not the individual α or β coefficients, are identified,

11. The test could not be performed where retirement was mandatory at age 65 or where no worker in a particular plan chose to retire at age 62.

Chapter 7

1. This decomposition is based on Euler's theorem, which in this context states that total utility is equal to the sum of two components, one equal to the amount of leisure consumed times the marginal utility of leisure and the other equal to the amount of income consumed times its marginal utility. The decomposition relies on the assumption that the underlying preference function is homogeneous of degree one.

2. The fact that tastes seem to be distributed roughly normally lends some support to the normality assumption adopted in estimating the linear regression models of chapter 5.

Chapter 8

1. In other words the hypothetical experiments alter the lifetime budget sets available to sample workers considering retirement during the 1970s.

Chapter 10

1. The methodology underlying this section is detailed in Fields and Mitchell (1985).

2. Our calculations in this chapter are limited to the LRHS because the BAS is less representative.

3. These rules are as published in the Social Security Administration's *Social Security Bulletin* and elsewhere.

4. The results reported in the text are for SOL simulations; MNL simulations were also evaluated for three of the four experiments. The two sets of results differed by less than one month in all cases: experiment A, +1.6 months in SOL versus +2.0 in MNL; experiment C, +0.2 months in SOL versus +0.3 months in MNL; experiment D, +2.9 months in SOL versus +3.6 months in MNL.

References

Aaron, Henry J. *Economic Effects of Social Security*. Washington, D.C.: Brookings Institution, 1982.

Amemiya, Takeshi. "Qualitative Response Models: A Survey." *Journal of Economic Literature* 19 (December 1981): 1483–1536.

Anderson, Kathryn H., and Richard V. Burkhauser. "The Effect of Actual Mortality Experience within a Retirement Decision Model," Working Paper 83-WO8. Vanderbilt University, Department of Economics and Business Administration, 1983.

Barnow, Burt S., and Ronald G. Ehrenberg. "The Costs of Defined Benefit Pension Plans and Firm Adjustments." *Quarterly Journal of Economics* 93 (November 1979): 524–540.

Bazzoli, Gloria J. "The Early Retirement Decision: The Influence of Health, Pensions, and Social Security." Ph.D. dissertation, Cornell University, 1983.

Bixby, Lenore. "Retirement Patterns in the United States: Research and Policy Interaction." *Social Security Bulletin* 39 (August 1976): 3–19.

Blinder, Alan S., Roger H. Gordon, and Donald E. Wise. "Reconsidering the Work Disincentive Effects of Social Security." *National Tax Journal* 33 (December 1980): 431–442.

Blinder, Alan S., Roger H. Gordon, and Donald E. Wise. "Rhetoric and Reality in Social Security Analysis—A Rejoinder." *National Tax Journal* 34 (December 1981): 473–478.

Boskin, Michael J. "Social Security and Retirement Decisions." *Economic Inquiry* 15 (January 1977): 1–25.

Boskin, Michael J., and Michael D. Hurd. "The Effect of Social Security on Early Retirement." *Journal of Public Economics* 10 (December 1978): 361–377.

Burbidge, John B., and A. Leslie Robb. "Pensions and Retirement Behavior." *Canadian Journal of Economics* 13 (August 1980): 421–437.

Burkhauser, Richard V. "The Early Retirement Decision and Its Effect on Exit from the Labor Market." Ph.D. dissertation, University of Chicago, 1976.

Burkhauser, Richard V. "The Pension Acceptance Decision of Older Workers." *Journal of Human Resources* 14 (Winter 1979): 63–75.

Burkhauser, Richard V., and Joseph F. Quinn. "Is Mandatory Retirement Overrated? Evidence from the 1970s." *Journal of Human Resources* 18 (Summer 1983): 377–358.

Burkhauser, Richard V., and Joseph E. Quinn. "Task Completion Report on the Relationship between Mandatory Retirement Age Limits and Pension Rules in the Retirement Decision." Final Report of the Urban Institute to the U.S. Department of Labor under Contract J-9-E-9-0065, June 1980.

Burkhauser, Richard V., and John Turner. "Can Twenty-five Million Americans Be Wrong?—A Response to Blinder, Gordon, and Wise." *National Tax Journal* 34 (December 1981): 467–472.

Burkhauser, Richard V., and John A. Turner. "Labor Market Experience of the Almost Old and the Implications for Income Support." *American Economic Review* 72 (May 1982): 304–308.

Burtless, Gary, and Jerry Hausman. "Double Dipping: The Combined Effects of Social Security and Civil Service Pensions on Employee Retirement." *Journal of Public Economics* 18 (July 1982): 139–159.

Burtless, Gary, and Robert Moffitt. "The Effect of Social Security on Labor Supply of the Aged: The Joint Choice of Retirement Date and Post-Retirement Hours of Work." Paper presented at the American Economic Association meetings, New York, December 1982.

Clark, Robert L., David T. Barker, and Steven R. Cantrell. "Outlawing Age Discrimination: Economic and Institutional Responses to the Elimination of Mandatory Retirement." Final Report to the Administration on Aging under Grant 90-A-1738, September 1979.

Clark, Robert L., and Thomas Johnson. "Retirement in a Dual Career Family." Final Report for the Social Security Administration under Grant 10-P-90543-4-02, 1980.

Clark, Robert L., and Joseph J. Spengler. *The Economics of Individual and Population Aging.* Cambridge and New York: Cambridge University Press, 1980.

Crawford, Vincent, and David M. Lilien. "Social Security and the Retirement Decision." *Quarterly Journal of Economics* 46 (August 1981): 505–529.

Cullinan, Paul R. "Health, Social Security and Retirement." Ph.D. dissertation, Syracuse University, 1979.

Diamond, Peter, and Jerry A. Hausman. "The Retirement and Unemployment Behavior of Older Men." In *Retirement and Economic Behavior.* Edited by H. Aaron and G. Burtless. Washington, D.C.: The Brookings Institution, 1984.

Employee Benefit Research Institute. *Retirement Income Opportunities in an Aging America: Income Levels and Adequacy.* Washington, D.C.: Employee Benefit Research Institute, 1982.

Employment and Training Report of the President, 1982. Washington, D.C.: Government Printing Office, 1982.

Feldstein, Martin. "Social Security and Private Savings: International Evidence in an Extended Life-Cycle Model." In *The Economics of Public Services.* Edited by M. S. Feldstein and R. P. Inman. London: Macmillan, 1977.

Fields, Gary S., and Olivia S. Mitchell. "Pensions and the Optimal Age of Retirement." Working Paper 27. Cornell University, Department of Labor Economics, March 1981.

Fields, Gary S., and Olivia S. Mitchell. "The Effects of Social Security Reforms on Retirement Ages and Retirement Income." *Journal of Public Economics* (1985, forthcoming).

Fields, Gary S., and Olivia S. Mitchell. "Economic Determinants of the Optimal Retirement Age: An Empirical Investigation." *Journal of Human Resources* 19 (Winter 1984): 245–262.

Flinn, Christopher, and James J. Heckman. "New Methods for Analyzing Structural Models of labor Force Dynamics." *Journal of Econometrics* 18 (January 1982): 115–168.

Fox, Alan. "Alternative Means of Earnings Replacement Rates for Social Security Benefits." In *Reaching Retirement Age.* Social Security Administration Report 47. Office of Research and Statistics, 1976.

Fox, Alan. "Earnings Replacement Rates of Retired Couples: Findings from the Retirement History Survey." *Social Security Bulletin* 42 (January 1979): 17–39.

Friedman, Joseph, and Jane Sjogren. "Assets of the Elderly as They Retire." *Social Security Bulletin* 44 (January 1981): 16–31.

Gordon, Roger H., and Alan S. Blinder. "Market Wages, Reservation Wages, and Retirement Decisions." *Journal of Public Economics* 14 (October 1980): 277–308.

Gordus, Jeanne P. *Leaving Early: Perspectives and Problems in Current Retirement Practice and Policy.* Ann Arbor, Mich. Institute of Labor and Industrial Relations, 1981.

Gustafson, Thomas A. "The Retirement Decision of Older Men: An Empirical Analysis." Ph.D. dissertation, Yale University, 1982.

Gustman, Alan L., and Thomas L. Steinmeier. "A Structural Retirement Model." Working Paper 1237. National Bureau of Economic Research, November 1983a.

Gustman, Alan L., and Thomas L. Steinmeier. "Partial Retirement and the Analysis of Retirement Behavior." *Industrial and Labor Relations Review* 37 (April 1984): 403–415.

Gustman, A., and Thomas L. Steinmeier. "Partial Retirement and Wage Profiles of Older Workers." Working Paper 1000. National Bureau of Economic Research, October 1982.

Gustman, Alan L., and Thomas L. Steinmeier. "Social Security Reform and Labor Supply." Working Paper 1212. National Bureau of Economic Research, October 1983b.

Hall, Robert. "The Importance of Lifetime Jobs in the U.S. Economy." *American Economic Review* 72 (September 1982): 716–724.

Halpern, Janice. "Raising the Mandatory Retirement Age: Its Effect on the Employment of Older Workers." *New England Economic Review* (May–June 1978): 23–35.

Hamermesh, Daniel S. "Social Insurance and Consumption: An Empirical Inquiry." *American Economic Review* 72 (March 1982): 101–113.

Hausman, Jerry A., and Daniel McFadden. "Specification Tests for the Multinomial Logit Model." Working paper 292. Massachusetts Institute of Technology, Department of Economics, October 1981.

Hausman, Jerry A., and David A. Wise. "A Conditional Probit Model for Qualitative Choice: Discrete Decisions Recognizing Interdependence and Heterogeneous Preferences." *Econometrica* 46 (March 1978): 403–426.

Hausman, Jerry A., and David A. Wise. "Social Security, Health Status, and Retirement." Paper presented at the National Bureau of Economic Research, Conference on Pensions, Labor, and Individual Choice, Dorado Beach, Puerto Rico, March 1983.

Heckman, James J. "Shadow Wages, Market Wages and Labor Supply." *Econometrica* 42 (July 1974): 679–694.

Heckman, James J., and MaCurdy, Thomas E. "A Life Cycle Model of Female Labour Supply." *Review of Economic Studies* 47 (January 1980): 47–74.

Hurd, Michael D. "The Effect of Social Security on Retirement: Results and Issues." Mimeographed. State University of New York and National Bureau of Economic Research, April 1983.

Hurd, Michael D., and Michael J. Boskin. "The Effect of Social Security on Retirement." Working Paper 659. National Bureau of Economic Research, April 1981.

Hurd, Michael D., and John B. Shoven. "The Economic Status of the Elderly: 1969–1979." Paper presented at the National Bureau of Economic Research, Conference on Research in Income and Wealth, Baltimore, December 1983.

Ippolito, Richard A. "Public Policy Toward Private Pensions." *Contemporary Policy Issues* (April 1983): 53–76.

Kiefer, Nicholas, and George Neumann. "An Empirical Job-Search Model with a Test of the Constant Reservation Wage Hypothesis." *Journal of Political Economy* 87 (February 1979): 89–107.

Kiefer, Nicholas, and George Neumann. "Wages and the Structure of Unemployment Rates." In *Workers, Jobs, and Inflation*. Edited by Martin N. Baily. Washington, D.C.: Brookings Institution, 1982.

Kotlikoff, Laurence J. "Social Security and Equilibrium Capital Intensity." *Quarterly Journal of Economics* 93 (May 1979): 233–253.

Kotlikoff, Laurence, and Daniel E. Smith. *Pensions and the American Economy*. Chicago: University of Chicago Press, 1983.

Lancaster, Tony. "Econometric Models for the Duration of Unemployment." *Econometrica* 47 (July 1979): 939–956.

Lando, Mordechai E., Malcolm B. Coate, and Ruth Kraus. "Disability Benefit Applications and the Economy." *Social Security Bulletin* 42 (October 1979): 3–10.

Lazear, Edward. "Retirement from the Labor Force." Mimeographed. University of Chicago, July 1983.

Lazear, Edward P. "Severance Pay, Pensions, and Efficient Mobility." Working Paper 854. National Bureau of Economic Research, February 1982.

Lazear, Edward. "Why Is There Mandatory Retirement?" *Journal of Political Economy* 87 (December 1979): 1261–1284.

Leonard, Jonathan S. "The Social Security Disability Program and Labor Force Participation." Working Paper 392. National Bureau of Economic Research, August 1979.

MacDonald, Glenn M., and Geoffrey Carliner. "A Theory of Optimal Retirement." Unpublished paper, University of Western Ontario, October 1980.

McFadden, Daniel. "Econometric Models of Probabilistic Choice." In *Structural Analysis of Discrete Data With Econometric Applications*. Edited by C. Manski and D. McFadden. Cambridge: MIT Press, 1981.

McFadden, Daniel. "Modelling the Choice of Residential Location." in *Spatial Interaction Theory and Planning Models*. Edited by A. Karlqvist et al. Amsterdam: North Holland Publishing Co., 1978.

McFadden, Daniel. "Quantal Choice Analysis: A Survey." *Annals of Economic and Social Measurement* 5 (Fall 1976): 363–390.

McFadden, Daniel. "Quantitative Methods for Analyzing Travel Behavior of Individuals." In *Behavior Travel Modeling*. Edited by D. Hensher and P. Stopher. London: Croom-Helm, 1979.

Mitchell, Olivia S., and Gary S. Fields. "Economic Incentives to Retire: A Qualitative Choice Approach." Working Paper 1096. National Bureau of Economic Research, March 1983.

Mitchell, Olivia S., and Gary S. Fields. "The Economics of Retirement Behavior." *Journal of Labor Economics* 2 (January 1984): 84–105.

Mitchell, Olivia S., and Gary S. Fields. "The Effects of Pensions and Earnings on Retirement: A Review Essay." In *Research in Labor Economics*, vol. 5. Edited by R. Ehrenberg. Greenwich, Conn.: JAI Press, 1982.

Mitchell, Olivia S., and Gary S. Fields. "Rewards for Continued Work: The Economic Incentives for Postponing Retirement." In Martin David and Timothy Smeeding, eds., *Horizontal Equity, Uncertainty, and Measures of Well-Being*. Chicago: University of Chicago Press for the National Bureau of Economic Research, forthcoming.

Munnell, Alicia. *The Economics of Private Pensions*. Washington, D.C.: Brookings Institution, 1982.

Munnell, Alicia H. "Social Security." *New England Economic Review* (July–August 1977): 16–43.

Parnes, Herbert, et al. *The Pre-Retirement Years*. Vol. 4. Washington, D.C.: Government Printing Office, 1974.

Parnes, Herbert S., ed. *Work and Retirement: A Longitudinal Study of Men*. Cambridge: MIT Press, 1981.

Parsons, Donald O. "The Male Labor Force Participation Decision: Health, Reported Health, and Economic Incentives." *Economica* 49 (February 1982): 81–91.

Quinn, Joseph E. "Micro-Economic Determinants of Early Retirement: A Cross-Sectional View of White Married Men." *Journal of Human Resources* 12 (Summer 1977): 329–346.

Quinn, Joseph E. "The Micro-Economics of Early Retirement: A Cross-Sectional View." Report to the Social Security Administration, Washington, D.C., 1975.

Reimers, Cordelia K. "The Timing of Retirement of American Men." Ph.D. dissertation, Columbia University, 1977.

Sammartino, Frank. "A Model of the Retirement Decision." Paper presented at the Labor Workshop, University of Wisconsin, Madison, February 1978.

Sammartino, Frank. "The Timing of Social Security Acceptance by Older Men." Unpublished paper. Office of Income Security Policy, Department of Health and Human Services, September 1980.

Schieber, Sylvester. *Social Security: Perspectives on Preserving the System*. Washington, D.C.: Employee Benefit Research Institute, 1982.

Schulz, James H. *The Economics of Aging*. Belmont, Calif.: Wadsworth, 1980.

Schulz, James, and R. Leavitt, as reported in R. Burkhauser and J. Quinn, "Pension Adjustment Factors by Industry." Mimeographed. June 1980.

Schwab, Karen, and Lola M. Irelan. "The Social Security Administration's Retirement History Study." In *Aging and Retirement: Prospects Planning, and Policy*. Edited by Neil G. McCluskey and Edgar E. Borgatta. Beverly Hills: Sage Publications, 1981.

Sheppard, Harold L., and Sara E. Rix. *The Greying of Working America: The Coming Crisis in Retirement Policy*. New York: Free Press, 1977.

Sheshinski, Eytan. "A Model of Social Security and Retirement Decisions." *Journal of Public Economics* 10 (December 1978): 337–360.

Small, Kenneth A. "Ordered Logit: A Discrete Choice Model with Proximate Covariance among Alternatives." Econometric Research Program Memorandum 292. Princeton University, December 1981.

Small, Kenneth A. "The Scheduling of Consumer Activities: Work Trips." *American Economic Review* 72 (June 1982): 467–479.

Social Security Administration. *Social Security Bulletin* 45 (September 1982).

Thompson, Lawrence. "The Social Security Reform Debate." *Journal of Economic Literature* 21 (December 1983): 1425–1467.

Tuma, Nancy, and Philip K. Robins. "A Dynamic Model of Employment Behavior: An Application to the Seattle and Denver Income Maintenance Experiments." *Econometrica* 48 (May 1980): 1031–1052.

Upp, Melinda. "Relative Importance of Various Income Sources of the Aged, 1980." *Social Security Bulletin* 46 (January 1983): 3—10.

Zabalza, Anthony, and D. Piachaud. "Social Security and the Elderly: A Simulation of Policy Changes." *Journal of Public Economics* 16 (October 1981): 145—170.

Zabalza, Anthony, Christopher Pissarides, and M. Barton. "Social Security and the Choice between Full-Time Work, Part-Time Work, and Retirement." *Journal of Public Economics* 14 (October 1980): 245—276.

Author Index

Subject Index